ROYAL HISTORICAL SOCIETY
STUDIES IN HISTORY
SERIES
No. 14

BRITAIN AND HER BUFFER STATE

The collapse of the Persian empire, 1890-1914

Other volumes in this series

BRITAIN AND HER BUFFER STATE

The collapse of the Persian empire, 1890-1914

David McLean

LONDON
ROYAL HISTORICAL SOCIETY
1979

The Society records its gratitude to the following, whose generosity made possible the initiation of this series: The British Academy; The Pilgrim Trust; The Twenty-Seven Foundation; The United States Embassy's bicentennial funds; The Wolfson Trust, several private donors.

The publication of this volume has been assisted by a further grant from the Twenty-Seven Foundation.

Printed in England
by Swift Printers Ltd
London E.C.1.

EVA KATALIN

CONTENTS

MAPS

PREFACE

In writing this book I have a number of debts to acknowledge. I am most grateful to the Marquess of Salisbury for his permission to quote from the Salisbury papers at Hatfield House. I am also grateful to Sir Patrick Browne who allowed me to consult the papers of his father, Professor E.G. Browne, at Thriplow in Cambridgeshire. At a later stage I received a generous grant towards the cost of publication from the Twenty-Seven Foundation. I have also received invaluable help in preparing this manuscript. First, from Professor D.C. Coleman who made a number of suggestions as to where further explanation on my part was necessary. Secondly, from Eva Gordon who caused me to revise much of the text and who greatly improved the written style. To dedicate this book to her is, in fact, the very least I can do.

David McLean

1

PERSIA AND THE WORLD'S 'SICK MEN'

Politically speaking, the late nineteenth century was a great age for 'sick men'. If nothing more they added a touch of romantic decay to a world dominated by trading and industrial giants. Civilizations in decline, or societies in disarray, capture the imagination in a way which the comparative statistics for coal and pig-iron production somehow never seem to manage. Wars were fought, empires built, and diplomatic tension generated when the great powers of Europe carved up the power vacuums of the world in the nineteenth century. Economic statistics, meanwhile, simply went on growing.

Politicians of the day liked the idea of 'sick men'. To speak of nations in decay was easy and of instant appeal to an audience of merchants, electors, or anyone else with whom high office necessitated contact. It also happened to be justified; in fact the list of the world's 'sick men' was quite a long one. Egypt, Morocco, Afghanistan, Turkey, Persia, China — all were areas where the indigenous regimes hovered on the verge of collapse. The governments of all these countries were weakened by internal unrest, by contact with European commerce and finance, by involvement with European politics, or by an ignorance and administrative inefficiency which left them helpless in the modern world. At one time or another either European control was imposed upon these areas or else the powers of Europe came to arbitrary agreements as to their destiny. Some historians have used the term 'imperialism' to describe this process: yet none of these nations was ever formally part of a European empire. The 'sick men' of the world really stood apart. They were neither colonies nor had they, in effect, the freedom and the independence of sovereign states. They survived in a world which measured nations according to manufacturing potential, financial wealth, and naval power, and in which they had all been found sadly wanting. Every one of them became a focus for the rivalry of the European powers in the late nineteenth or early twentieth centuries. Their geographical positions and their incapacity for self-defence drew them inevitably into the orbit of international diplomacy in which they had but little say and over which they had absolutely no control.

Britain was always a party to the rivalries which developed. She disputed influence in Afghanistan with Russia, in Morocco and Egypt with the French, in Persia with Russia and later with Germany, and in Turkey and in China with virtually everybody. With an empire which stretched world wide almost everywhere had an importance in the context of global strategy. Morocco flanked the entrance to the Mediterranean. Egypt controlled the sea-route to India through the Suez Canal. Turkey commanded the Bosphorus and the Dardanelles and had long been used to keep Russian naval squadrons bottled in the Black Sea. Afghanistan and Persia became barriers between the southward spread of Russia and the frontiers of the Indian empire. In China alone were there no considerations of imperial defence; there the British defended their political and commercial interests in the Yangtsze Valley and tried to prevent Russia from absorbing Manchuria in the north. Always the British had to bear in mind their position as a great world power and their international prestige. The fact that political rivalry had developed was usually enough to make the outcome a matter of importance.

The 'sick men' were distinguished not only by their political status and by the international rivalry which centred on them. They were distinguished too by the fact that the nineteenth-century traditions of British foreign policy were considerably modified in respect of them. British activity in Persia between 1890 and 1914 illustrates the way in which established attitudes gave way to the requirements of a new era in diplomacy. In no respect was this more apparent than in the changing relationship of political and economic factors, and in the new association between British officials and diplomats on one hand and private financial interests on the other. Such changes were by no means confined to Persia. Trends which emerge from the study here emerge just as strongly from those of British policy in China, in Turkey, and for all the world's 'sick men'. But Persia was the case of change *par excellence.* The general aim of British officials remained the same throughout those years; the means employed to reach it represent, in many ways, a revolution in the conduct of foreign policy.

Unquestionably the British saw themselves as the harbingers of peace, prosperity, and justice in the nineteenth century, and the standards of official practice which had evolved in the decades prior to 1890 reflected, by and large, those virtues. For one thing, it was an axiom of policy that the British government did not meddle in the internal affairs of other nations. For another, officials believed that private economic enterprise was not something with which they should concern themselves other than to ensure that no discrimination was exercised against British trading and commercial interests. These were the guidelines handed down from Lord Castlereagh to Sir Edward Grey. These were the general principles which British diplomats and officials at the Foreign Office always acknowledged.

The doctrine of non-interference in the internal affairs of other nations was well established. In an age dominated by liberal ideas, and by the Liberal party in British politics, departures from this rule would not escape the sternest of rebukes. No government in England could deny that the sovereign integrity of foreign nations had to be respected. No government would lightly undertake any action to the contrary. And as if high principles were not enough the British had learned their lesson from the mistakes of the past. The expedition to Argentina in 1806 and Lord Aberdeen's attempt to decide the outcome of the war in the Uraguay by means of naval action in the River Plate in 1845 were conspicuous by their failure. There was ample evidence at hand that non-interference was the wisest and the safest course. Furthermore, intervention implied responsibility and British governments throughout the nineteenth century took the view that they had responsibility enough. Britain kept out of the civil war in China between 1850 and 1864 on that basis. Officials had no wish to assume the task of picking up the pieces if the Manchu dynasty collapsed.

The same was true for Persia. The British government had neither the inclination nor the means to impose its own administration on any part of the country. It wished to do nothing which weakened the central government at Tehran. The Shah was, in 1903, 'the ruler whose independence we have bound ourselves to support'.[1] The Foreign Office still claimed in 1910 that 'His Majesty's Government had no wish to intervene in the internal affairs of Persia'.[2] There was limits to which British diplomats could go in dealing with a foreign ruler. Propriety was all-important. The British Minister at Tehran assured his chief in 1895 that the Shah would do anything provided that the price was right. An annual subsidy from the British treasury could produce the reforms, the commercial expansion, and the administrative improvements which the Foreign Office wanted to see; but he presumed, quite correctly, that no such measures would be entertained in London. Even in their foreign policy British governments were answerable to a Parliament which was zealous in its guarding of the public purse. What is more, Parliament could always produce a handful of brilliant, pious, or eccentric individuals, gifted in oratory and skilled in debate, to champion the cause of a weaker nation in any struggle against British domination.[3]

1 Minute by Lansdowne on Hardinge to Lansdowne, 10 June 1903, F.O. 60/667.

2 Grey to Marling, 10 May 1910, F.O. 371/954.

3 See, for instance, Lord Stanhope's tirade against the government when gunboats blew open the path for British trade at Canton in 1840: *Hansard* (Lords) 3rd ser. LIV, 1-26, 12 May 1840. Palmerston's government was defeated in the House of Lords in 1857 by Cobden's resolution condemning the outbreak of

Yet there were far-flung frontiers to defend and local circumstances which sometimes required exceptions to this norm. 'Sick men', moreover, often provided just such circumstances. Twice in the nineteenth century a British expedition occupied Kabul when the Amir of Afghanistan refused to toe the line which the Government of India had drawn him. Keeping Afghanistan free from Russian control necessitated military invasion on those occasions and diplomatic suasion throughout the century. In Egypt even Gladstone's Liberal government felt obliged to impose a British administration in the early 1880s. The safety of the Suez Canal and the security of India were factors which overcame his initial reluctance to do so. Constantinople was the scene of a diplomatic tussle to control the Porte from the 1820s onwards. In view of all this the principle of non-interference may seem rather meaningless. It might be said to have applied to the civilized states of Europe, but the extent of Britain's empire meant that the government was always watchful of the affairs of Asiatic nations which lay beyond its frontiers. Yet the guide-line as such still operated. Unless it was strictly necessary British politicians and officials would shun the effort and the expense of a forceful policy anywhere in the world and they would always maintain that they were anxious to uphold such a virtuous tradition in foreign relations.

The second tenet of British policy prior to 1914 was that the government did not meddle in the world of economic enterprise.[1] Here was a principle which if taken at face value was inalienable. Throughout the nineteenth century British governments seemed to hold themselves aloof from commerce and from financial investment overseas. Men who engaged in such activities, and those who placed their money in such speculations, did so entirely at their own risk. It was not the function of the diplomatic service to bale out British subjects when their money was lost. Nor was it the duty of the government to give advice. Persia again was no exception. The Foreign Office had no wish to press the interests of British financiers upon the Persian government. As Lord Salisbury, the Foreign Secretary, explained in 1891: 'We do not wish to assume the invidious position of urging vigorous measures in order that foreigners may make money'.[2] When it was put to him in 1892 that he might try to interest the house of Rothschild in a Persian loan the reply was that no overture of that sort could possibly be made.

hostilities with China, *Hansard* (Lords) 3rd ser. CXLIV, 1155-1238, 24 February 1857. See also G.M. Trevelyan, *The Life of John Bright* (London, 1913) p. 258.
1   The best statement of this principle is D.C.M. Platt, *Finance, Trade, and Politics in British Foreign Policy 1815-1914* (Oxford, 1968).
2   Salisbury to Kennedy, 6 September 1891, Foreign Office Confidential Print [6359].

The Foreign Office was always suspicious of private enterprise. Salisbury warned the new British Minister in 1891 that 'our commercial adventurers are very much on the watch, and would be very glad to convert the legation into an agency for pushing British speculations in Persia'. [1] Invariably, officials believed, financiers tried to trick the Foreign Office into giving unmerited support. When speculators found that their investment did not pay a case was always made out for diplomatic assistance in gaining compensation from foreign régimes. The Persian Bank Mining Rights Corporation was one such offender. The Permanent Under-Secretary noted in 1893 that they 'went into business in Persia at their own risk and if they expected to find the same order and security which is looked for in Europe, it is their own fault if their anticipations were not realised'. [2] There was sound reasoning behind this official disinterest. If the British government gave advice or offered its support some obligation to the firm in question might be incurred. On this the Foreign Office and the Treasury were adamant. The British government could never accept responsibility for private enterprise abroad.

This was expressed in a number of ways. Diplomatic assistance was not usually available. Nor did the British government pay out subsidies to enable British firms to cope with foreign competition. Most strikingly, perhaps, the government refused to guarantee the payment of interest to British bondholders on loans to foreign states. Subsidies and guarantees required the approval of Parliament; this was hardly ever given and very seldom asked for. When the Foreign Office was approached about the possibility of a subsidy for road construction in Persia in 1892 the reply was that the House of Commons would never sanction such a use of public funds in a country not under British protection. In the same year the Persian government was told that a direct loan from the British treasury was out of the question since Parliament would never consent. In 1895 and 1898-9 the British government refused to guarantee loans to Persia 'on Parliamentary grounds'. [3] An official explained as late as 1905 why this principle was one to be encouraged: 'if we begin guaranteeing loans to Persian officials it is difficult to see where we shall stop'. [4] Similarly the Foreign Office could not undertake the task of negotiating terms for British bankers. It was not the government's job to act as agents for financial enterprise.

1 Salisbury to Lascelles, 6 October 1891, *Salisbury Papers,* A/71.

2 Minute by Currie on Persian Bank Mining Rights Corporation to Foreign Office, 26 October 1893, F.O. 60/576.

3 Memorandum by Sanderson, 28 February 1900, F.O. 60/630.

4 Minute by Gorst on Hardinge to Lansdowne, 13 July 1905, F.O. 60/714.

The British government had no control over the affairs of private interests. This was what the Foreign Office always claimed, and in an age when *laissez-faire* was the dominant strand in economic thinking one might well have expected it to be so. In 1912 the Foreign Office still stressed that it had no check on the operations of the British Imperial Bank in Persia. Salisbury had declared, twenty years earlier, that he lacked any control in respect of the British Tobacco Regie in the country. There was no formal channel of communication between the Foreign Office and the City. Financiers could, and sometimes did lend capital abroad contrary to the wishes of the government. Furthermore, it was accepted practice that British officials never discriminated between individual firms. Where support was given it was given to economic enterprise in general. When the Persian government was looking for a loan in London in 1910 the Foreign Office confirmed that 'we have no right to support one British group against another'.[1] There would be an outcry at home if the government strayed from this fundamental measure of fair play. In Persia, as elsewhere, British officials made it plain that economic interests should be something quite distinct from the higher plane of political and diplomatic activity. Again the British government set its own standards for behaviour and again those standards were very high.

They were too high in fact. It was not possible for the government of the world's greatest industrial and financial power to keep out of commercial enterprise overseas altogether. Naturally the government felt some obligation to smooth the path for British traders. It negotiated free-trade treaties in the 1830s and 1840s on their behalf. Indeed British diplomats abroad would always press the case for free and unrestricted commerce upon a foreign government. Lord Lansdowne, the Foreign Secretary in 1902, put it very succinctly to the Persian Prime Minister when he visited London in that year: 'we are essentially a commercial people', he remarked, 'and commercial interests are largely represented in our Parliament'.[2] No government in the nineteenth century could afford to be insensitive to the needs of Britain's expanding commerce and industry. Even if it was not the government's job to find new markets for British exports it could reasonably be expected to prevent existing openings for trade from being closed, and this was what it had to do in China in 1839. Similarly, exceptions to the general rule on overseas loans, though rare, can be found. The Treasury promised support for a Moroccan loan in 1861 and it guaranteed loans to Greece in 1833 and 1898 and to the Turkish government during the Crimean War. Nor was the refusal of diplomatic assistance to British invest-

1   Minute by Norman on Marling to Grey, 29 June 1910, F.O. 371/958.
2   Lansdowne to des Graz, 18 August 1902, C.P. [8214].

ments abroad quite as rigid as officials implied. Formal representations to a foreign government were certainly to be avoided if possible, but unofficial support for British firms was a feature of nineteenth-century diplomacy. The Foreign Secretary in 1907 referred to 'diplomatic support, good offices, or whatever other varieties of diplomatic support there may be'.[1]

By the end of the century, indeed, it was obvious that politics and economic activity could no longer be considered apart. Increasingly economic affairs took on a political importance and the Foreign Office had to act accordingly. It promised support for loans under negotiation to the Persian and Chinese governments in 1898, it lent money to the Persian government in 1903 and 1904, and it supported a Persian loan project in 1910. From the 1880s Parliament granted subsidies for British steamships to ply the Tigris and Karun Rivers at the head of the Persian Gulf. Clearly, too, there were now many contacts, both personal and professional, between government officials and the great financial houses in the City: the efforts of the Foreign Office to organize a loan for China in 1895 are evidence enough of that.[2] In the 1900s the relationships between British officials and the operations of the Hong Kong and Shanghai Bank in China, and the National Bank of Turkey in the Ottoman empire, are striking examples of the way in which finance and politics became tightly interwoven. It might be asked if the British government's supposed abstention from any dealings with economic enterprise overseas, particularly after 1890, is a valid principle by which to judge its Persian policy. That principle, however, was one to which officials claimed adherence up to 1914 and it is not therefore unreasonable that their actions should be assessed accordingly.

* * * * *

These standards of non-intervention in the domestic politics of other nations and in the affairs of British businessmen abroad had to be set against the background of local circumstances. Nowhere was that more important than in Persia. British observers consistently remarked upon the peculiarities of this oriental society. First, the destitution of the country. Secondly, the value of such intangible elements as face and prestige and the significance which was attached to the personalities of the individuals on the spot. Thirdly, the way in which political authority became a function of financial domination. In these respects, of course, Persia was not unique. These were the hall-marks of any

1 Grey to Nicolson, 1 April 1907, *Nicolson Papers*, F.O. 800/339.
2 D. McLean, 'The Foreign Office and the First Chinese Indemnity Loan, 1895', *Historical Journal* 16 (1973).

ailing nation; these were the factors which distinguished her as one of the world's 'sick men'.

As for the country's destitution, Persia's decline had long been apparent. Throughout the nineteenth century the British witnessed in Persia all the qualities of eastern despotism. The Shah's kingdom was one of faded glories: the mainstream of history and of economic progress had long sinced passed it by. By the end of the century the disappearance of Persia as an independent state seemed to be imminent. The country was totally defenceless against Russian pressure from the north. The Persian army was nothing more than an undisciplined mob and hopelessly ill-armed. The only troops upon which the central government could rely for maintaining order in and around Tehran were those of the Persian Cossack brigade (about 1,500 men) under the command of Russian officers. When a British mission arrived at Tehran to confer the Order of the Garter on the Shah in 1903 a sentry at the imperial palace presented arms with a broken table leg. Small wonder British observers doubted Persia's capacity for survival. The British Minister described the Shah in 1905 as 'weak, capricious, and almost totally uneducated', and surrounded by a group of courtiers whose sole interest was plundering the public revenues.[1] It was a great mistake, he had remarked earlier, to treat Persian statesmen as if they had any regular lines of policy. Government offices were freely auctioned, payments to officials and to the army were always in arrears, corruption and bribery were everywhere outstanding. The central government exercised little more than a token authority. The priesthood controlled the people; provincial governors, once they had bought their posts, devoted their energies to extorting the maximum profit from the areas which they administered. Persian officials, seeing the end in sight, drew the conclusion that they had best fill their own pockets in preparation.

The extravagance of the Shah and his court held out little hope for financial improvement. Even the fact that most of the revenues collected through taxation, customs duties, and rents never reached the central exchequer could not curb it. The budget deficit, in 1901 for instance, was £300,000. A further £350,000 was already owed to foreign banks, and the visit which the Shah was planning to Europe for the summer of 1902 foretold another large annual deficit.[2] Quite understandably the fortunes of a Grand Vizier could depend upon his success at raising loans from abroad. Yet there were still those who cherished the idea of a stronger and more prosperous Persia. Sir Mortimore Durand, the

1   Hardinge to Grey, 23 December 1905, C.P. [8730].
2   Hardinge to Lansdowne, 6 November 1901, F.O. 60/645.

British Minister between 1894 and 1900, was one of them. Persia's trade had increased in the past twenty years, a regular postal and telegraph system had been established, and the country in the 1890s had no sizable national debt. By Asian standards, he concluded, Persia was by no means hopelessly lost. Drawing on his experience in the Government of India, Durand remarked that areas of India in an even worse condition had been saved by the imposition of effective administration under British auspices. If only the British government could reach some agreement with Russia about the introduction of reforms in Persia, and some common policy to preserve the country's territorial integrity, anything might be possible. Few shared even this qualified optimism. For most British officials Persia was 'incurably rotten',[1] and the disintegration of the central régime was only a matter of time. But just how long that might take, how long it would be before Persia ceased to be an independent state, was very difficult to predict. Persia had been badly governed for generations. The mass of the population tilled the soil and paid exhorbitant taxes as they had always done. There would still need to be some impulse, either internal or from outside, to push the tottering régime at Tehran over the brink of total collapse.

Secondly, the British were well aware of the value of prestige in Persia. It mattered greatly how the legation was treated by Persian officials. As one of the legation staff put it in 1908: 'all officials who have served in the East know how largely our position there depends on credit'.[2] The British government, therefore, should never be seen to back down. The Russians understood this principle very well. The slightest reverse could be most damaging to political reputation. The respect of the Persians, and their co-operation in all matters, was pro-portionate to the firmness with which they were treated; Russian diplomacy with its strong-arm tactics scored heavily against the more patient and conciliatory attitude which the British tended to adopt. 'Orientals', the British Minister in Tehran reported in 1901, 'are most impressed by outward signs of power'.[3] Unless those signs were present Persian officials would assume that the power itself had gone, and they would throw in their lot with the nation whose diplomats acted with the greatest verve and bluster and whose threats of stronger action were the most convincing. It was a mistake to tolerate any want of respect from an Asiatic regime. The Minister judged that 'a little wholesome fear, mixed with confidence in our intentions' would put Anglo-Persian

1   Memorandum by Curzon, 12 April 1896, C.P. [6765].

2   Smart to Browne, October 1908, *Browne Papers,* file: letters from Persia 1905-9.

3   Hardinge to Lansdowne, 2 April 1901, C.P. [7730].

relations on a far more satisfactory basis than hitherto.[1] The Viceroy of India, complaining of a lack of determination in Britain's Persian policy in 1903, put it bluntly to the Foreign Secretary that 'a good show of the boot now and then is very essential'.[2]

Economic matters also carried prestige. The strength of British trade, and the extent to which the economic development of the country was in the hands of British concessionaires, would determine Britain's standing both at Tehran and in the areas concerned. Even the most harmless institutions might have political implications. A school which the Germans had established at Tehran and which they wished to enlarge in 1908, for instance, was not viewed favourably by the Foreign Office in London. The scheme should be nipped in the bud, the British legation advised. A British hospital in 1911 was much encouraged. An official observed that 'any foundation which is calculated to increase our influence in Persia is good'.[3] Prestige being a factor in the East which the British therefore took seriously the character of the men whom the British government sent out to Persia would obviously be of considerable importance.

Among the qualities required for service in Persia brainpower did not figure prominently. Durand, for instance, was described by one of the consular staff as an ideal chief. Durand's career as a diplomat was to prove a dreadful failure. In Persia, however, he made a great impression, not because of any power of incisive intellect but because 'he is as thoroughly imbued with pride of race as every Briton ought to be'.[4] Everyone in the 1890s remembered the success which Sir Henry Drummond-Wolff had had in Tehran between 1888 and 1890 and attributed it largely to his exuberant personality and to the extraordinary influence which he had been able to exercise over the Shah. A later Minister, Sir Arthur Hardinge, explained the value of such strength of character. In their qualities and vices the Persians were rather like the Irish, he tactlessly informed an Irish Foreign Secretary. 'It is very little use to argue in the dry light of pure reason; you have to enter, in both cases, into his peculiar sympathies, to make large allowance for the shams and vanities on which he lives, and you will do more by a little cordiality, a little gush, and, I would add, a little blarney, than by the most serious and sustained reasoning'.[5]

1   Memorandum by Durand, 27 September 1895, C.P. [6704].
2   Curzon to Lansdowne, 3 April 1903, *Curzon Papers, mss. eur.* F111/162.
3   Minute by Norman on Thompson to Foreign Office, 9 March 1911, F.O. 371/1188.
4   Sykes to Curzon, 9 April 1895, *Curzon Papers,* F111/62.
5   Hardinge to Lansdowne, 16 July 1905, *Lansdowne Papers,* F.O. 800/138.

The men for the consular posts in Persia also had to be well chosen. The legation praised the political Resident in the Gulf as a man who was of the greatest benefit to Britain's position there. The Resident got on well with the trucial chiefs, he was tactful, and yet he was also firm and consequently much respected. The British agent who was sent into the province of Seistan was another such case. The Viceroy had selected him for this particular post on the grounds that his 'swagger and self-assurance' were the very qualities which were required. It would do a great deal of good that the Seistan agent was not reserved and timorous like most Englishmen, the Viceroy remarked, but that he 'swells himself out a little, and struts before the world'.[1] The Persians were apt to take a man at his own valuation, and that valuation should therefore be a good one. The same principle applied to all British institutions operating in Persia, not just to the diplomatic and consular services. The Imperial Bank of Persia was often criticized for the fact that it employed 'cheap and nasty foreigners' in Persia instead of true Englishmen who were far better suited to dealing with orientals and their devious ways.[2]

Thirdly, it became plain to the British that economic strength and political power in Persia were closely related. The Board of Trade acknowledged in 1904 that 'commercial influence is a useful political weapon, and the extension, or decline, of trade with Persia has a deeper interest to the Russian and the British empires than the simple gain or loss of profitable markets'.[3] It was not just that the extension of commerical enterprise enhanced political prestige. Trade also meant prosperity for Persia, and prosperity was a possible precursor of the political strength and stability which the British deemed to be necessary if the country was to survive as an independent unit. In consequence the British government was always attentive to the requirements of British trade in Persia. It pressed for the opening of the Karun River to foreign navigation for decades prior to its ultimate success in 1888. Later it encouraged the construction of British roads and took such steps as it could to keep them open. Economic concessions were also politically important. In a country where the presence of the central régime was negligible railways, roads, telegraphs, mining rights, irrigation works, and shipping services all became means by which foreign footholds could be established. Economic interests frequently required protection. They were a ready pretext for military occupation and they were always a justification, in the eyes of the controlling power, for claiming

1   Curzon to Hamilton, 24 July 1901, *Hamilton Papers,* mss. eur. D510/8.

2   Yate to Hardinge, 11 September 1897, *Hardinge Papers,* vol. 2.

3   H.W. MacLean's report to the Board of Trade, 1904, enclosed in Board of Trade to Foreign Office, 25 March 1912, F.O. 371/1433.

special interests and a right to interfere in the region. Nowhere was economic enterprise free from political implications. Its development in Persia, quite naturally, was one of the major considerations of British policy between 1890 and 1914.

Because financial interests gave an opportunity for political activity by foreign powers, the British government took the view that the less other foreigners were involved in the economic affairs of Persia the better. This applied particularly to economic concessions in the south. In addition, the British attached great importance to controlling the customs revenues of the ports of the Persian Gulf. These revenues were derived largely from British trade, they formed one of the most regular sources of income for the central régime, and they were an obvious security which could be offered by the Persian government in return for money borrowed from abroad. In 1903 their value was about £180,000. By 1907-8 the figure had risen to £227,000, at a time when the total amount collected from all Persian customs was £709,000.[1] Lord Salisbury warned the Persian government in 1897 that interference by foreigners could not be tolerated and that it would be 'a grave error of policy' to pledge the customs revenues as security for non-British loans.[2] In October 1897 the British gained an assurance from the Shah that no foreign management of the customs revenues of the Gulf ports would be allowed — a pledge which the Foreign Office successfully enforced right up to 1914.

That economic and political matters became inseparable in Persia merits yet wider illustration. There was the question of power over the government at Tehran by providing it with financial assistance. In a general sense the greater Britain's investment in Persia the greater her stake in the future of the country. If the central regime were to break down the British government would benefit in any division of the spoils with Russia by the fact that Persia was largely indebted to British capitalists. In 1903 the British Minister spelled out the advantages of lending money in no uncertain terms. 'The more we get her into our debt the greater will be our hold and our political influence over her government', he advised the Foreign Office. 'Once the day of liquidation comes, the greater Persia's financial obligations to us, and the more equal their distribution between Russia and ourselves, the stronger will be our moral claim to an authoritative voice in the settlement'.[3] Loans meant political authority at the Persian court, just as they meant

1 Hardinge to Lansdowne, 14 May 1903, C.P. [8378]; and Foreign Office minute on Barclay to Grey, 30 April 1909, F.O. 371/717.

2 Salisbury to Hardinge, 15 October 1897, F.O. 60/601.

3 Hardinge to Lansdowne, 18 July 1903, C.P. [8399].

political authority at Constantinople and at Peking. The provision of funds for the ailing regime at Tehran was one of the principal issues on which British and Russian diplomacy clashed in the late 1890s and early 1900s.

2
BRITAIN AND RUSSIA IN PERSIA

Left alone, Persia would have quietly disintegrated. Its passing as a sovereign state would scarcely have affected the course of eastern civilization. But Persia was not to be left alone. European rivalry and imperial expansion cast their long shadows across the tattered fabric of the Persian empire. It was largely geography which determined Persia's role in international affairs. Squeezed between the frontiers of the two great imperial powers of the nineteenth century her position was inevitably insecure. To the north lay Russia; to the south-east lay the Indian sub-continent − the show-piece of Britain's wealth and global power. Persia formed part of the belt of neutral territories which separated these Asiatic empires: Afghanistan and Thibet were similarly placed. All three were the focus of intrigue and suspicion between Britain and Russia. It was to be a settlement of their rivalry in these three areas which constituted the Anglo-Russian Convention of August 1907. Persia continually felt the pressure of Russia on her northern frontier. There was a relentless momentum to Russia's southward expansion. One day, it seemed, Persia would be reduced to the status of a frontier province of the Russian empire in just the same way as the other territories of Central Asia had been.

The Persian empire had once included the Caspian Sea. Gradually Russia had brought the area around it under her control and in 1874 the trans-Caspian region was added to the Russian empire as an administrative unit. In the mid nineteenth century Russia had prepared her ground in Central Asia. Forts were built, towns were taken, and areas of steppe were annexed. The three Central Asian Khanates of Khokand, Bukhara, and Khiva had been absorbed by 1873. All became vassal states. Nominally independent, in fact they were firmly under the thumb of the Russian government. In the 1880s a new phase of expansion was under way. The resistance of the Turkmen was broken at Geok-Tepe in 1880 and the Merv Oasis submitted to Russian rule in 1884. The Russian railway network was extended into Central Asia. The trans-Caspian railway was begun in 1880; it was extended to Merv by 1886 and to Samarkand in 1888. In 1895 Tashkent was linked to the Russian railway system. In 1900 the extension from Merv to Khushk was finished which brought the Russian railhead up to the frontier of Afghanistan. These developments were a constant worry to the Government of India, as indeed was the completion of the important Orenburg-Tashkent railway in 1904.[1] In the twenty years after 1863 the relative

1   Kitchener to Minto, 23 May 1906, enclosed in Minto to Morley, 12 June 1906, I.O. L/P&S/10/125, 1907, file: 3278.

positions of Britain and Russia in Central Asia changed considerably. In 1863 1,700 miles of mountains and desert had separated the Russian frontier and the outermost area of British India. By 1883 that mileage was reduced by half, due almost entirely to the expansion of Russia.[1]

Russian imperial expansion in the nineteenth century had a profound impact on British observers. In cases of doubt Russia would always be attributed with the most sinister motives. Where the extension of Russian territory was successfully executed this was held up as evidence that British mistrust was fully justified. Anglo-Russian rivalry, of course, was a prominent feature of international relations throughout the nineteenth century. British and Russian diplomacy were continually opposed — particularly after the early 1830s when the struggle began over the fate of the Ottoman empire and command of the Straits. Paramountcy at Constantinople was the important issue; this was linked with Britain's determination to preserve the Turkish empire as a barrier against Russian expansion towards the Mediterranean and to safeguard the overland route to India. In later decades British policy was to limit Russian influence in the Balkans and to counter Russia's designs in the Far East, where the province of Manchuria and even the Chinese court at Peking were gradually being brought under Russian sway. Central Asia was only one part of the world where Britain and Russia found themselves in conflict in the nineteenth and early twentieth centuries. Persia, in its turn, was but one of the territories of Central Asia which neither power could afford to let pass under the control of its adversary.

There was some superficial agreement between Britain and Russia over Persia in the nineteenth century. By an understanding in 1834 both powers had bound themselves to maintain the existence of the country. These assurances were subsequently reaffirmed. On paper this was an admirable arrangement; but no one in Britain, or indeed in India, placed any faith in Russia's general expressions of good will. Few men could have disagreed with the conclusion of the War Office in 1902 that when it suited Russia's purpose she would ignore any number of treaties or conventions and respect only superior military force as a limiting factor on her ambitions. British suspicions stemmed from their ideas about the worth of Persia to Russia. First, it was a market for Russian manufactures. The British had no difficulty in appreciating that; nor had they any doubt that Russia's intention was to close as much of Persia as possible to British trade and to establish a commercial

1 R.L. Greaves, *Persia and the Defence of India 1884-92* (London, 1959), p. 60. The background to Russia's advance in Central Asia is well covered in R.A. Pierce, *Russian Central Asia 1867-1917* (California, 1960), pp. 17-45.

monopoly for Russian enterprise. Secondly, Persia was for Russia, as it was for Britain, strategically important; indeed it was in the realm of Russia's global strategy that the real significance of Persia lay. Taking Persia, the Far East, and the Ottoman empire together Russia's consistent ambition was to gain access to warm water ports. These would be fortified and they would serve as naval bases from which Russia would be in a position to disrupt British interests throughout Asia. Persia in itself was thought to be of limited value. What the Russians really wanted was a right of way through the country to an outlet on the Persian Gulf. Just as they seized Port Arthur from China in 1898 and rapidly converted it into a first rate naval station so they might now take either Chahbar or Bunder Abbas.[1]

British officials agreed, then, as to the general aims of Russian expansion. Some even believed that Russia had forced a promise from the Persian government that in the event of an emergency Russian troops might pass through the country and occupy one of the southern ports. There was similar agreement about Russian methods; again the British reviewed Russian activity in a global context. Russia would not invade Persia by force: that was not her way. As at Constantinople, at Lhasa, at Peking, and in the Khanates of Khiva and Bukhara, Russian tactics were to keep the existing régime in power but to reduce the reigning sovereign to a state of complete dependence on Russian troops and Russian money for his throne.[2] 'She will endeavour to advance her interests by artifice and bluff, rather than by actual war', the War Office predicted in 1903.[3] Military occupation would be a costly business, particularly for a nation whose financial resources were always strained and whose military power was already occupied in holding down an empire which stretched from the Caspian to the China seas. The British feared a gradual absorption of Persia under Russian control. For that purpose Russia would try to keep the régime at Tehran just strong enough to survive but weak enough to have to obey the dictates of Russian diplomacy.

Russia's attempt to direct the Persian government rested principally on three factors: geography, diplomacy, and finance. Russia had the advantage of a long frontier with Persia on which she could at any moment mobilize her forces. It would be an easy matter for Russian troops to cross the frontier, to apply direct pressure on the Persian

1   Spring-Rice to Hardinge, 27 July 1899, *Hardinge Papers*, vol. 3; and Spring-Rice to Villiers, 23 August 1899, *Villiers Papers*, F.O. 800/23.

2   Government of India to India Office, 4 February 1904, I.O. L/P&S/10/122, 1907, file: 3128;   and memorandum by Balfour, 22 April 1904, I.O. C.I.D. L/Mil/5/729, 1903-4, no. 46.

3   War Office memorandum, 9 April 1903, F.O. 60/673.

government, or to support some pro-Russian claimant to the Peacock throne. Though lengthy occupations were expensive, Persian officials could never be sure when Russia would deem the cost to be worthwhile, or whether, if they tried to call her bluff, Russia might not overrun the northern provinces for the sake of her prestige. The British drew the obvious parallel with the unfortunate position of the Manchu court at Peking. Military pressure, both in Persia and in China, did not require actual invasion. The threat alone was usually sufficient when directed at a weak and ignorant régime, unsure of any assistance from outside.

Russian diplomacy was all the stronger for the threat which could be substantiated. By comparison the British could threaten to seize a few ports or islands in the Gulf but, unlike his Russian counterpart, the British Minister at Tehran was never in a position to intimate the possibility of action inland. Yet Russian diplomacy did not rest solely on the menace of military intervention. The Russian legation exercised considerable pressure on officials in the Persian government by bribery and by support, and Russian consuls and political agents in the provinces often managed the local governors by similar methods. Russia forced through a major loan contract in 1900 by virtue of her hold over the Sadr-i-Azam (Prime Minister). With his help, too, the Russian legation pressed the Shah to agree to the extension of Russia's embargo on railway construction in Persia until 1910. Russia's influence in court circles at Tehran led the British Chargé d'affaires to accuse the Persian government of being the paid servants of Russia and of caring for nothing but taking the bribes which were lavishly offered.

The line between bribery and finance could be a fine one. Any loan to Persia meant a substantial cut for the officials through whose hands the money passed. Legitimate finance, though, remained the more important means by which the Russians confirmed their hold over the Persian government, particularly since severe political conditions were attached to any loan. Financing the central government was part of Russia's policy to establish a 'veiled protectorate' in Persia, the British Minister remarked.[1] Russia would subjugate the country commercially and financially. She would isolate Persia from all other foreign contacts, she would appropriate the Shah's revenues as loan security, she would obstruct any economic progress in the country, and then, having reduced the Persian government to complete dependence on Russia for financial support, she would rule the country by means of Russian advisers to the Shah. 'Notwithstanding all the talk about their embarrassed domestic position', he warned, 'their treasury can always find money for advances to decaying Eastern governments, as a cheaper

1   Hardinge to Lansdowne, 10 June 1905, C.P. [8559].

mode of conquest than war'.[1] Russia's attempt to establish a monopoly of financial aid, coupled with the constant threat of a military occupation of northern Persia, were 'the two pincers of the forceps in which she holds and by which she squeezes the Shah'.[2]

Russia also increased her influence in Persia by more general economic means. The extension of her trade was one of them. For this purpose the Russian government tried to negotiate a tariff agreement with Persia in 1902, aimed to discriminate heavily against British trade while favouring its own. Similarly, the Banque des Prets was backed by the Russian treasury as a means of fostering Russian commercial enterprise and of advancing money to the Persian government. Russia strengthened her position in northern Persia by financial investment too. The Enzeli harbour scheme on the shores of the Caspian in the mid 1890s was a prominent example. So was the road network which the Russians pushed forward from Enzeli to Resht and on to Tehran and which, of course, meant that the Persian capital was rendered more accessible to military operations from across the frontier. Understandably the British were quite content that railway construction in Persia was postponed for many years by way of the Russo-Persian agreement of 1890 (renewed in 1900). By threat, by diplomacy, and by control of the principal arteries of communication Russia, it seemed, was gradually consolidating her position in the north of Persia and bringing officials both of the central government and in the provinces increasingly under her direction.

When British officials debated policy, or when they took such steps as they thought necessary to protect British interests in the south of Persia, they did so with the knowledge that Russia, not Britain, was the dominant force at Tehran. The British had bemoaned their waning influence in Persia from an early date. In 1817 the legation had written to Castlereagh that 'our influence in Persia . . . is likely to sink under the weight which Russia will acquire at this court'.[3] Yet it was only towards the end of the century that the growth of Russian power seemed irreversible. The failure of the Tobacco Regie in the early 1890s was something of a turning point. The Shah had granted a monopoly of the sale and handling of tobacco in the country to a British syndicate but under pressure from the priesthood, and faced with riots and disorder inflamed by the intrigues of Russian agents, he had been forced to cancel it despite protests from the British legation.

1 Hardinge to Lansdowne, 20 July 1903, *Lansdowne Papers*, F.O. 800/138.
2 Hardinge to Lansdowne, 19 July 1904, *Lansdowne Papers*, F.O. 800/138.
3 Quoted in J.B. Kelly, *Britain and the Persian Gulf 1795-1880* (Oxford, 1968), p. 167.

Britain's inability to provide a loan for the Persian government in 1898-9 proved a further setback. Both episodes were felt to be considerable blows to British prestige. Persian officials were beginning to suspect that Britain had lost interest in Persia or, even worse, that the British government had accepted defeat in the struggle against Russia's gradual advance. The hands of successive British Ministers in Persia were effectively tied. The qualifications for the job, one incumbent explained, were that 'he would have to be contented, married to a contented wife and not too ambitious; and indifferent to the rapid decline of British influence'.[1] If the British legation were too energetic in pressing its claims, or in its efforts to advise the Persian government, the only result would be that Russia would tighten her grip even further. 'Russia can do anything she chooses', the Chargé d'affaires lamented in 1900, 'and England is simply a sort of Aunt Sally for the Persian government to throw stones at'. 'I have been here in a time of unexampled decay of British influence', he concluded on leaving Persia in February 1901.[2] The British were rightly pessimistic about the future of Persia and uncertain about the measures which should be employed to protect their interests in the south. The advantage of geography and the ease with which the Russian government could mobilize its financial resources ensured that the diplomatic struggle over Persia would not be fought on equal terms. The British reconciled themselves to the fact that they might not succeed in Persia beyond a holding operation against the spread of Russian power into the central and southern provinces. The legation summed up Russia's successes in 1900: 'it is simply big batallians and money bags which have done the trick'.[3]

Persia was of no immediate value to Britain. The British had no desire for territorial acquisition, nor any real wish to become involved in the affairs of the Persian empire. In the first place British interests were simply commercial. The expansion of Britain's trade throughout the world in the nineteenth century had spread the tentacles of her commercial empire even to so unpromising a country. In relation to her total overseas trade Britain's commercial links with Persia were small. In an age when Britain's exports were valued in hundreds of millions of pounds those destined for the Persian market were counted only in hundreds of thousands. The bulk of British exports to Persia was cotton goods. The traffic in reverse comprised mainly opium, dried

1   Spring-Rice to Hardinge, 25 July 1900, *Hardinge Papers*, vol. 3.

2   Spring-Rice to Hardinge, 7 March 1900, *Hardinge Papers*, vol. 3; and letter by Spring-Rice quoted in S. Gwynn, *The letters and Friendships of Sir Cecil Spring-Rice* (London, 1929), I, 331.

3   Spring-Rice to Hardinge, 25 July 1900, *Hardinge Papers*, vol. 3.

fruit, and woollens. British exports to Persia rose in value from the 1870s onwards. The total was only £50,000 in 1875, but nearly £170,000 in 1879. By 1898 the figure had reached over £300,000; by 1903 it was over £400,000, and by 1907 it was £700,000. After 1907 it declined sharply due mainly to the political unrest in Persia. In 1908 the figure was under £500,000. In 1909 only £355,000 worth of British exports entered the country. Trade with Britain, though, was not the whole picture. The flow of goods between Persia and the Indian empire was not unimportant. From 1893 to 1909 the value of goods entering Persia from India always exceeded that of exports direct from Britain. In the favourable years of 1893, 1894, and 1898 the total value of goods passing from India to Persia topped £1 million. The total trade of the British empire, both exports to and imports from Persia, was estimated at £3½ million in 1898, £2,700,000 in 1903, over £4 million in 1907-8, and £5 million in the peak year of 1911.[1]

Britain was not even Persia's principal trading partner. British trade accounted for only 24 per cent of Persia's total external commerce in 1900-1: that of Russia accounted for nearly 57 per cent.[2] Russian trade almost doubled in the ten years after 1888. Until 1902 the value of Russian imports from Persia tended to exceed that of her export trade. Russian exports, however, were the thing which attracted the greatest attention in British commercial circles. In 1893 their value was £1,195,000. By 1898 it had risen to almost £1,800,000. In 1907 the value of Russian exports to Persia just failed to reach the figure of £3 million. After 1911 the figure was consistently over £5 million. In 1913 Russian imports from Persia were also valued at well over £4 million. Russia's total trade with Persia by then was valued at nearly £12 million per annum. The principal commodities were sugar, tea, cotton goods, linen, metals, and glass. There was no question, therefore, of Britain being able to claim commercial predominance in Persia. Russian goods entered Persia overland and supplied the markets of the northern provinces. Even though Russian trade with Persia never constituted more than 4 per cent of Russia's total foreign trade, in terms of a commercial stake in Persia Russia's was obviously greater than that

---

1 The figures for British and Indian trade are based on the consular reports for the trade of Persia 1880-1914: in particular, Parliamentary Papers, LXXI (1880); LXXXV (1887); LXXVII (1889); CI (1899); XCV (1904); XCI (1905); XCIV (1911); XCIII (1914); LXXIV (1914-16). R.P. Churchill, *The Anglo-Russian Convention of 1907* (Cedar Rapids, 1939), pp. 223-7. Board of Trade to Foreign Office, 13 September 1910, enclosed in India Office to Foreign Office, 5 November 1910, F.O. 371/951. Memorandum by Law, 11 June 1902, C.P. [8160].

2 War Office memorandum, 14 October 1902, printed with memorandum of 4 October 1902, F.O. 60/657.

which the British could claim.[1] When the British talked of paramountcy in trade it was to the south and to the waters of the Persian Gulf that they referred.

In the realm of finance things were much the same. The amount of British capital invested in Persia was a minute percentage of the vast total which flowed out from London in the century before 1914. Though the Persian government relied heavily on foreign borrowing from the 1890s onwards the sums in question were seldom large. In 1911 Persia's total foreign debt was estimated by the supervisor of the government's finances at £6 million. On the surface this was not oppressive. The total revenues which reached the Persian government were calculated in 1903 at nearly £1¼ million per annum.Had there been a semblance of honest and efficient administration in the country that figure would have been much greater. The repayment of foreign creditors would have been comparatively easy — if, indeed, incurring such obligations would have been necessary in the first place. Persia's chief obligations were to the Russian government. Of the £6 million debt in 1911 nearly £3¼ million had been taken in Russian government loans. All told the Russians had invested about £7 million in Persia by 1905 in loans, roads, harbour works, and the Banque des Prets. In her two major loans to Persia, in 1900 and 1902, Russia had supplied Persia with nearly £3½ million. By comparison debts to British creditors were small. In 1905 Persia's outstanding obligations to Britain totalled only a few hundred thousand pounds. The British government itself was an important creditor. By two advances, in April 1903 and September 1904, it had provided the Shah with £300,000. In 1912 the British government advanced a further £140,000. By the end of that year Persia's indebtedness to H.M.G. was over £450,000 [2]

The principal British financial institution in the country was the

---

1   This assessment of Russian trade with Persia is based upon Churchill, p. 223. Board of Trade to Foreign Office, 6 March 1903, *Curzon Papers,* F111/358. Board of Trade to Foreign Office, 13 September 1910, enclosed in India Office to Foreign Office, 5 November 1910, F.O. 371/951. M.L. Entner, *Russo-Persian Commercial Relations 1828-1914* (Florida, 1965), pp. 9, 62, 66. Parliamentary Papers, XCIII (1914).

2   These figures for Persian finance are taken from F. Kazemzadeh, *Russia and Britain in Persia 1864-1914* (New Haven, 1968), p. 473. Minute by Ritchie on Foreign Office to India Office, 25 August 1911, I.O. L/P&S/10/11, 1903, file: 4122. Hardinge to Lansdowne, 14 May 1903, C.P. [8378]. Minute by Maxwell on des Graz to Lansdowne, 1 August 1902, F.O. 60/660. Foreign Office memorandum to the Cabinet, 10 March 1905, Cabinet Papers 1900-05, F.O. 899/5 no. 41. War Office memorandum on Persia by the General Staff, 1905, *Curzon Papers,* F111/387. Minute by Mallet on Townley to Grey, 25 November 1912, F.O. 371/1435. Foreign Office memorandum on Persian loans, 27 November 1912, F.O. 371/1711.

Imperial Bank of Persia. By the terms of its concession this was the state bank of Persia, founded in 1889. Its paid up capital was £650,000 and up to a third of that figure could be advanced to the Persian government at any one time. The Bank was the sole agency for issuing notes in Persia; it dealt in foreign exchange, discounted bills, and it lent to institutions and to individuals alike. Its profits were not spectacular but at least they existed. In very good years, such as 1890-2 and 1909-13, they exceeded £50,000. As far as the British government was concerned the most important aspect of its operations was its loans to the Persian government. 'These, politically,' the legation at Tehran remarked in 1903, 'are of very great value'.[1] By 1895 the debt to the Bank was already £135,000: by 1898 it was £200,000, and by 1907 over £450,000. The Bank was the agency through which the British government made its advances to Persia. The Bank's only competitor in Persia, at least until 1910, was the Russian Banque des Prets. Other British firms in Persia comprised the trading houses in the Gulf, the most important of which was the Euphrates and Tigris Steam Navigation Company controlled by the redoubtable H.F.B. Lynch.

The trade in the Gulf was a sea-borne trade. Here the primacy of British enterprise was obvious. In 1900-1 just over one million tons was entered and cleared at Persian ports: nearly 900,000 tons were British. In 1902 90 per cent of shipping in the Persian Gulf flew the British flag. The imports and exports of the Gulf ports between 1895 and 1897 totalled over £17 million of which foreign trade comprised over £12 million. Of that £12 million more than 80 per cent was trade with Britain or with British India. But though the British were supreme in the trade of the south of Persia the sums in question were still small. The commercial department at the Foreign Office observed, quite rightly, that 'compared with our world trade it is quite insignificant'.[2]

The Gulf, however, meant something more to the British than simply a statistic of foreign trade. In the course of the nineteenth century the Government of India had assumed a responsibility for protecting commerce and maintaining law and order in the region, and the Residents whom it had stationed in the Gulf since 1820 possessed a political

1 Hardinge to Lansdowne, 29 March 1903, C.P. [8378]. The information concerning the Bank is also drawn from Imperial Bank of Persia to Foreign Office, 21 August 1895, F.O. 60/570. Gordon to Sanderson, 29 January 1898, F.O. 60/601. Imperial Bank of Persia to Foreign Office, 20 July 1907, C.P. [9296].

2 Minute by Law on War Office to Foreign Office, 26 April 1911, F.O. 371/1178. The statistics for the trade of the Persian Gulf are also drawn from Churchill, p. 217. Government of India to India Office, 21 September 1899, C.P. [7456]. War Office memorandum, 14 October 1902, printed with memorandum of 4 October 1902, F.O. 60/657.

authority among the local Arab (trucial) chiefs. Justly, perhaps, the British looked back with pride on their achievement. The Persian government was told in 1902 that it benefitted greatly from Britain's position there. The waters off the Persian coast had been cleared of pirates and the British navy policed the lanes along which trade and commerce flowed. The Gulf enjoyed the peace and progress of the Pax Britannica and Britain claimed with confidence the right to be sole arbiter in its affairs.[1]

Yet by the early twentieth century British officials viewed the Persian Gulf with growing anxiety. The supremacy, both commercial and political, to which they were accustomed seemed to be passing. Ottoman power began to challenge British authority at the northern end. After 1902 Germany pushed ahead with her Bagdad railway project which the British feared would terminate at an outlet on the Gulf. The British were extremely sensitive to these pressures and to the growth of foreign commerce in Gulf waters. German trade developed in the late 1890s. The value of German exports to Persia stood at £22,000 in 1897 and rose to £62,000 in 1901. By 1904-5 that figure had topped £130,000, by 1910-11 £250,000, and by 1913-14 £500,000. The total value of German trade with Persia stood at over £600,000 in 1913-14.[2] The trade of the Gulf took on a political dimension. An Under-Secretary at the Foreign Office observed in 1898 that 'commercial interests are the familiar precursor to political claims'.[3] Officials in London were convinced that the German government paid handsome subsidies to the Hamburg-America line which operated steamship services between Hamburg and the Gulf. That firm seemed to be reasonably successful in the first three years of its operations before 1909. British shipping interests informed the India Office in 1913 that the company had entered the Persian Gulf trade under the auspices of the German government with a view to establishing a footing there for

1 Lansdowne to Hardinge, 6 January 1902, C.P. [8085]. British activity in the Persian Gulf has become, in itself, a field for historical research. The major works for the nineteenth and early twentieth centuries are Kelly, op.cit; and B.C. Busch, *Britain and the Persian Gulf 1894-1914* (California, 1967). There is also a good chapter in G.S. Graham, *Great Britain in the Indian Ocean 1810-50* (Oxford, 1967), pp. 219-62. See also R. Kumar, *India and the Persian Gulf Region 1858-1907* (London, 1965).

2 Board of Trade to Foreign Office, 6 March 1903, *Curzon Papers*, F111/358. A general background to German activity in Persia is given in B.G. Martin, *German-Persian Diplomatic Relations 1873-1912* (The Hague, 1959). Statistics for German trade are also taken from Parliamentary Papers, XCIV (1911); XCIII (1914); LXXIV (1914-16). W.O. Henderson, 'German Economic Penetration in the Middle East 1870-1914'. *Economic History Review* 18 (1948) 64.

3 Memorandum by Curzon, 19 November 1898, C.P. [7067].

German interests and for the Bagdad railway.[1] The Foreign Office, five years earlier, had noted with alarm the efforts of the Hamburg-America line to form a large combine with British shipping interests. The Permanent Under-Secretary was sure that the German firm had lost money in the past, that repeated losses would soon drive it out of business in the Persian Gulf, and that its overtures to British shippers were a desperate bid for survival. He admitted that the Foreign Office was 'trying hard to prevent' the combination from ever succeeding.[2] The commercial department rightly drew the conclusion in 1911 that the trade of the Gulf 'is more important politically than commercially'.[3] The British wished to keep the Persian Gulf a *Mare Clausum*. If Russia or Germany established coaling stations or naval bases there it 'would be a thorn in our side', the War Office decided, and the distribution of British naval resources would have to be reconsidered. 'The injury they could do us would be serious and lasting', the Foreign Office concluded.[4] The defence of the empire rested on Britain's naval power, and in waters which gave access to the Indian Ocean the supremacy of that power should never be in doubt.

But British interests reached beyond the Persian Gulf. The whole of the country was important as a neutral state between India and Russia. More specifically, the south-east corner of Persia attracted the attention of the British and Indian authorities. The Seistan basin was one of the gates to India. Unless the Russians advanced through Herat in Afghanistan their only route for an invasion of India lay through the Persian province of Seistan. The importance of keeping that province free from Russian control was therefore enormous. If Russia became dominant there not only would an area of the greatest strategic value be lost, but Russia would be in a position to conduct intrigues designed to disrupt both Britain's presence in Afghanistan and her handling of the turbulent tribes on the Indian frontier. A Russian railway from her trans-Caspian line via Meshed into the province would be a further disaster. Russia's forward frontier, in that case, would effectively be advanced by over 300 miles and her ability to concentrate an army within striking distance of India would be considerably increased.[5] Seistan was a source of con-

1 Inchcape to Holderness, 29 December 1913, I.O. L/P & S/10/366, file: 4424.

2 Hardinge to Barclay, 15 March 1909, *Hardinge Papers,* vol. 17.

3 Minute by Law on War Office to Foreign Office, 26 April 1911, F.O. 371/1178.

4 War Office memorandum, 14 October 1902, printed with memorandum of 4 October 1902, F.O. 60/657. C.C. Davies, *The Problem of the North-West Frontier 1890-1908* (Cambridge, 1932), pp. 185-6. Memorandum by Curzon, 19 November 1898, C.P. [7067].

5 Military report on Persian Seistan, 1902, *Curzon Papers,* F111/378 p. 7. The

stant worry to British and Indian officials until 1907. It was a matter of great relief that when Persia was partitioned into spheres of influence in that year Seistan fell within the British boundary. Persia, then, was originally an Indian interest. Lord Salisbury had remarked in 1889: 'were it not for our possessing India we should trouble ourselves but little about Persia'.[1] In the years which lay ahead Persia became a pawn in the diplomatic struggle between the European powers. Nonetheless, Persia still meant the defence of India and any diplomatic compromise with Russia could only be at India's expense.

The nineteenth century background to British policy in Persia is amply covered. The principles on which that policy rested are well known.[2] The British had taken some interest in the country at the beginning of the nineteenth century though the fate of Persia was not recognised immediately as of any real significance. The Government of India during the Napoleonic Wars had no fear of a Russian attack on India across Persia. Britain's principal concern was to stop hostilities between Russia and Persia so as to free the Russians to fight the French in Europe. Not until 1807 did a member of the government in London acknowledge that Britain had an interest in seeing the sovereignty of the country maintained.[3] Russia's wars with Turkey and Persia in the 1820s caused anxiety to British and Indian officials. The value of Persia as a first line of defence for India was recognised in 1835 when Palmerston informed Lord Durham, the Ambassador at St. Petersburg, that 'the independence of Persia is a great object to us'.[4] By the time of the Anglo-Persian War in 1856-7 this principle had been firmly established. Although Kharaq and Bushire in the Persian Gulf were seized the British had no intention of dismembering the Persian empire or of allying themselves with any of the tribes of the interior.

Persia's independence, however, always seemed to hang by a thread. It needed to be strengthened by the economic development of the country and by the introduction of sound reforms. This was an import-

importance of Seistan to Indian interests is dealt with in Greaves, *Persia and the Defence of India,* pp. 17-19; and Churchill, pp. 220-1.

1   Quoted in Greaves, *Persia and the Defence of India,* p. 25.

2   By far the major works are Greaves, *Persia and the Defence of India;* and Kazemzadeh, *Russia and Britain in Persia.* Other useful studies are A.P. Thornton, 'British Policy in Persia 1858-90 I and II', *English Historical Review* 69 (1954) and 70 (1955). R.L. Greaves, 'British Policy in Persia 1892-1903 I and II' *Bulletin of the School of Oriental and African Studies* 28 (1965). For the early part of the nineteenth century see also Graham, pp. 262-82.

3   E. Ingram, 'An Aspiring Buffer State: Anglo-Persian Relations in the Third Coalition 1804-07', *Historical Journal* 16 (1973) 531.

4   Quoted in Kelly, pp. 287-8.

ant aspect of British policy. If the Shah wanted British help he had first to help himself. The British had no hesitation in pointing out the measures which were necessary. The extension of trade, especially in the south, was perhaps the most important of these; the British, from the 1840s onwards, saw the opening of the Karun River to foreign navigation as a prerequisite for this. The natural resources of the country had to be developed too. Internal security was to be improved. The worst abuses in Persian administration had to be abolished. Tax and revenue collection were to be put on a proper basis with a far tighter control by the central government. Here, the British believed, lay the secret of economic prosperity — prosperity which could provide the means for training and equipping an efficient Persian army, which in turn could lead to political stability and would render the country a more effective bulwark against Russian expansion. Communications had to be improved and foreign capital and expertise had to be imported for the purpose. The British set great store by a railway linking Tehran with the Gulf littoral and by the development of roads which would distribute the trade of the Karun region. 'Until some road or railway is made we can not help Persia', Salisbury remarked in 1888.[1] Throughout the nineteenth century the British government shunned the Shah's request for a firm commitment to defend his domains; it relied instead upon these measures of self-help to bolster the country's independence. There was no undue optimism. Salisbury was to admit quite frankly in 1891 that he felt all efforts 'for stiffening Persia' might come to nothing in the end.[2] But for most of the time there was no urgency about Persian affairs. The attention both of British politicians and of the Government of India focussed principally on Afghanistan until the end of the 1870s. The Government of India, of course, took a great interest in the area beyond its north-west frontier. Elaborate defence plans were drawn up. An agency was established in Baluchistan in 1877 and a British expedition was sent into Afghanistan in 1878. Afghanistan was the traditional buffer state which would protect the passes on the north-west frontier. Only when the British lost faith in their ability to preserve it as such did they turn their serious attention to the Persian empire.

The British had to watch Persia more closely by the 1870s. After the submission of the three Central Asian Khanates to Russia, Tehran was promoted to the front line in the clash between British and Russian diplomacy. Persia was left as the last fragment of a once great zone of neutral territory which had stretched across Central Asia. In 1879

1 Salisbury to Drummond-Wolff, 27 June 1888, *Salisbury Papers,* A/71.
2 Quoted in Greaves, *Persia and the Defence of India* p. 182.

Salisbury tried to negotiate an agreement with the Persian government which would have strengthened Britain's position considerably. In 1888 Sir Henry Drummond-Wolff was sent out to Tehran to increase Britain's influence with the Shah and to put Anglo-Persian relations on a far more positive footing. More than that, Salisbury wanted an agreement with Russia by which both powers would confirm Persia's integrity and would undertake to work for the introduction of reforms and economic progress. Salisbury and Drummond-Wolff were the great advocates of the buffer policy in Persia. They wanted Persia strong, and to help achieve that end they wanted British economic enterprise to become established. Drummond-Wolff was certainly successful. The Karun was opened to foreign trade, the Imperial Bank of Persia was founded, an assurance as to railway concessions in the south was given, and the tobacco monopoly was gained. In addition Wolff tried to get British commercial and financial houses to take an interest in the country.[1] But Wolff's influence passed as quickly as it had come. The revival of British authority at Tehran had depended too much on his forceful personality and when his health failed in 1890 he had to be recalled. None the less the mission remained an important landmark. Salisbury had clearly established the principle that Persia should be maintained as a buffer state, and the struggle to do so was to dominate British policy for the next twenty-five years.

That idea occurs time and again in the writings of British officials after 1890. The survival of Persia remained the ambition of the Foreign Office as late as 1914. The Government of India in 1901 saw Persia as one of the 'buffers' that separated the Indian empire from the Asiatic possessions of Britain's rivals.[2] In 1902, when British policy was being seriously reconsidered, the Foreign Secretary explained the role which Persia was to play. It had long been one of the principles of British policy to encourage and to strengthen the states which lay beyond the frontiers of India. The hope was that 'we should find in them an intervening zone sufficient to prevent direct contact between the dominions of Great Britain and those of other great military powers'.[3] The India Office too recognized the need to maintain 'a weak buffer state between two strong empires'[4] – a description applicable both to Persia and to Afghanistan. References to the need to support the unity of Persia were legion. The 'buffer state' was something of which British officials

1 Drummond-Wolff to Salisbury, 18 April 1888, *Salisbury Papers,* A/70.

2 Memorandum by Curzon, 28 October 1901, enclosed in India Office to Foreign Office, 19 March 1902, C.P. [8085].

3 Lansdowne to Hardinge, 6 January 1902, C.P. [8085].

4 Hamilton to Curzon, 16 February 1900, *Curzon Papers,* F111/145.

were acutely aware. By the 1890s it remained to be seen how capable they were of securing it: or whether, as one British politician ruefully reflected, 'our pretentions and policy in that country are based upon an order of things that is passing away'.[1]

1 Cabinet memorandum by Lord George Hamilton, 27 December 1901, *Hamilton Papers*, F111/58.

3

THE GREAT DEBATE

The best that can be said of British officials concerned with Persia in the 1890s and early 1900s is that they agreed to differ. Seldom can there have been such chaos over policy. The rapid growth of Russian power in Persia in the 1890s required a reappraisal of British attitudes. It called into question the feasibility of preserving Persia as a buffer state at a time when Britain's military and financial resources were already strained by the Boer War and by the Boxer Rebellion in China. Policy needed some redefinition, and, as never before, it had to conform to the limits of what was possible. Those limits were themselves a matter for controversy. The Persian debate was a reassessment of Britain's role as a world power, and a reconsideration by the Government of India of frontier defence. It stands out too as a remarkable display of recrimination between the British and Indian governments, between government departments in London, and between the individuals at home and those in Persia.

In fairness, it would have been surprising had there not been some divergence of opinion over Persia. Throughout the nineteenth century Persia had been a shared responsibility between London and Calcutta. The scope for argument was all the greater for the fact that money was involved — in particular the payments which were necessary to maintain the legation at Tehran and the consulates dotted around the country. Running the diplomatic mission had been delegated to the East India Company between 1823 and 1835. Thereafter the Crown retained control though departmental responsibility was unsettled. In 1858 the Tehran legation was transferred to the jurisdiction of the India Office. From 1860 onwards the Foreign Office took charge, but the Government of India continued to pay half the cost of the British diplomatic establishment in Persia.

Understandably the Imperial government and the Government of India viewed Persia from different standpoints. For India it was a matter of frontier defence. The 'buffer state' existed for the benefit of India and not as a factor in European diplomacy. For the Foreign Office Persia was really a diplomatic backwater. Tehran merited only a legation, not an embassy. A man might have to serve there for a few years while awaiting a more comfortable appointment in Europe; but the climate, the state of the country, and the need to deal with orientals made it a spot to be avoided. Certainly the appointment to Tehran mattered rather more after the mid 1890s, but first rate men at the legation were rare before 1914. Persia only really became important for the Foreign Office when international tensions focused upon it. The home government saw Persia primarily as part of Anglo-Russian rivalry on a global scale.

By the 1890s the question of responsibility for Persia was no longer in doubt. The British government paid for and appointed the legation staff. The Minister at Tehran was answerable to the Foreign Secretary in London. The consular service, in turn, was under the authority of the legation. India's responsibility was primarily for the Persian Gulf and in particular for the political Resident stationed at Bushire. The India Office in London had no policy of its own for Persia. It freely admitted that the Government of India depended entirely upon the Foreign Office for guidance.[1] The debate between London and Calcutta was not, then, a dispute as to where authority lay. The conflict was a clash of individual views and personalities, and these were conditioned only to a limited extent by the positions of high office held by the men in question.

Just as some difference of opinion was inevitable between Whitehall and Calcutta so too between the Foreign Office and the legation at Tehran. The men on the spot saw Russian expansion in northern Persia at close quarters. They were often brought into contact with 'cruder and franker expressions of Russian views and aspirations than those formulated by the cautious and conciliatory statesmen who served as the mouthpieces of Russian policy in London and St. Petersburg'.[2] Diplomatic and consular officers lamented the fact that the Foreign Office did not seem prepared to do anything in Persia. The British Minister complained in February 1899 that a lengthy memorandum which he had submitted suggesting important changes remained virtually unanswered.[3] In 1899 and again in 1907 the legation complained of being seriously short staffed.[4] In 1900 the Chargé d'affaires boldly advised the Foreign Secretary that the Persian service should be 'put on a business footing, and not organised like a circus'.[5]

The Foreign Office in the late 1890s was not receptive to appeals for increasing and radically reorganizing the consular establishment in the

1 Bayley to Sanderson, 27 December 1892, *Sanderson Papers,* F.O. 800/1.
2 Hardinge to Lansdowne, 10 June 1905, C.P. [8559].
3 Durand to Lee-Warner, 16 February 1899, *Durand Papers,* mss. eur. D727/6.
4 Spring-Rice to Hardinge, 20 December 1899, *Hardinge Papers,* vol. 3; and Smart to Browne, 22 April 1907, *Browne Papers,* file: letters from Persia 1905-09.
5 Letter by Spring-Rice, quoted in Gwynn, I op.cit. p.318.

country. In 1902 the Minister at Tehran bemoaned the fact that almost everyone in London regarded Persia as an unmitigated bore. His scheme to improve Britain's influence in Persia by persuading the Shah to visit London and to meet British politicians had received not the slightest encouragement. The King seemed determined to upset the Shah by refusing to confer the Order of the Garter upon him, and no one of Cabinet rank expressed any wish to meet him because the visit would be inconvenient during the shooting season. To cap it all, the Shah's reception in England would be a very meagre one compared to that which he would receive at St Petersburg; without doubt the Shah would return to Persia far more impressed with the power of Russia to harm him than with the capacity of Britain to protect him. 'No wonder the Russians always beat us', the Minister continued, 'they are in earnest and we are not'.[1] In a fit of despair the Chargé d'affaires wrote in 1900 that 'with the present management I had almost rather leave the service of the Foreign Office altogether, or indeed of the government'.[2] Disagreement with his superiors, in July 1902, led to the Minister's application to be posted elsewhere.

From 1900 to 1905 the British Minister in Persia was Sir Arthur Hardinge. Hardinge had his own ideas about Persia which were not always shared by others. The authorities in London often disapproved of his diplomacy. Hardinge was deemed to be inconsistent and his advice on various matters was thought to be unrealistic. Lord George Hamilton, the Secretary of State for India, considered him 'a very tiresome representative' who made no effort to carry out the instructions which he received.[3] The weakness of his position at Tehran *vis-à-vis* his Russian counterpart seemed to be affecting his judgement. Moreover, he was inclined to treat Persian officials with undeserved civility. The fact that he was unhappy at his post gave rise to the suspicion that he might make his work as light as possible until such time as he was transferred. Even the Foreign Secretary seemed reluctant to defend him. In 1903 he had to admit that the legation staff had not the aptitude for the work required.[4] Hardinge's staunchest critic, though, was the Viceroy of India – Lord Curzon. Hardinge and Curzon were old friends: but even the memory of their years together at Eton, at Balliol, and as Fellows of All Souls could not stem the condemnation which flowed from Curzon's pen. Hardinge had no appreciation of what was

1 Hardinge to Curzon, 5 July 1902, *Curzon Papers*, F111/179.
2 Letter by Spring-Rice, 20 September 1900, quoted in Gwynn, I op. cit. p. 324.
3 Hamilton to Curzon, 7 May 1903, *Hamilton Papers*, mss. eur. C126/5.
4 Lansdowne to Curzon, 24 April 1903, *Curzon Papers*, F111/154.

needed east of Suez. His policy was one of 'wheedling the Atabeg and murmuring honeyed things to the Shah', as a result of which both took advantage of his generous nature.[1] In Curzon's view, Hardinge had never grasped the realities of the Persian problem. Even when the Foreign Office, the India Office, and the Government of India reached agreement, Hardinge was sure to be out of line and arguing for something else. Hardinge himself saw things in a different light. He criticized the inaction of the British government and he took exception to the Viceroy's tactics. Curzon was impatient and knew nothing about the need for compromise in diplomacy. It was impossible for a British diplomat to bully the government in Persia in the same way that the Viceroy was able to lay down the law in areas like Nepal and Afghanistan. Curzon was too accustomed to getting his own way quickly. In Persia, Hardinge remarked, patience and personal relations were the order of the day. When Hardinge and Curzon planned to meet in the Persian Gulf at the end of 1903 the Foreign Secretary certainly foresaw the prospect of some fiery exchanges: 'I should doubt whether it was big enough to hold them both!'[2]

Hardinge and Curzon could sink their differences on one thing. Both were scathing of the men with whom they had to deal in London. The British government, they claimed, had no policy in Persia: it simply drifted with the course of events. Action was only taken when it was too late. Hardinge and Curzon were not alone in this view. Certainly the India Office, and even some of the junior officials at the Foreign Office, concurred. The blame was put squarely on the shoulders of the man who was Prime Minister between 1895 and 1902 and Foreign Secretary from 1895 to 1900 — Lord Salisbury. Under his control the British government had allowed Russia to establish herself at Port Arthur on the Pacific coast and to increase her political influence at Peking, at Constantinople, in Central Asia, and, of course, in Persia. Curzon's criticism was perhaps the most telling of all. Curzon owed his rapid rise in public life almost entirely to Salisbury's patronage yet even he could not contain his disappointment. He did not believe that Salisbury would make the slightest effort to save Persia. As one who had served as Parliamentary Under-Secretary at the Foreign Office from 1896 to 1899 he spoke with some knowledge of Salisbury's administrative abilities and of the working of the institution. 'There are no settled principles of policy in relation to any part of the world; and everyone, from the exalted head down to the humblest

---

1   Curzon to Godley, 10 April 1902, *Curzon Papers*, F111/161.
2   Minute by Lansdowne on Hardinge to Lansdowne, 19 July 1904, *Lansdowne Papers*, F.O. 800/138.

clerk, sits there anxiously waiting to see what will turn up next'.[1] Moreover, Salisbury had been the dominant influence at the Foreign Office since the late 1870s; the traditions which had prevailed there under his guidance would not be swept away overnight.

Recrimination was only one side of the coin. Constructive suggestions certainly existed. Personal reproaches, in fact, throw little light on the wider issues which were being considered. They serve rather as an indication of how imperfectly the men concerned with Persia understood each other's motives, and how headstrong some of those individuals tended to be. Even the criticisms of the Foreign Office, by and large, were undeserved. In matters of policy the British divided into two principal camps. There were those who were determined to stand by Persia as a buffer state and to take a firm line against Russian encroachments. Alternatively, there were those who believed that this was impracticable and that the 'buffer state' would have to be abandoned in favour of a more tangible hold on south-east Persia and the southern end of the Persian Gulf.

To some extent, the maintenance of Persia as a buffer state depended on the willingness of the British government to provide finance. Only by advancing money to the Persian government, or by helping private financiers to lend, could the British government exercise any diplomatic influence. If the Shah were obliged to turn to Russia for the means with which to preserve his throne then Russian tutelage at Tehran was unavoidable. After 1890 the Shah was always in search of money. He borrowed £500,000 from British financiers in 1892 and negotiated unsuccessfully for larger sums between 1896 and 1899. A big Russian loan of £2,400,000 in 1900, however, was the decisive move: principally because Persia was forbidden to borrow elsewhere abroad until the money was repaid, but also because of the prestige and weight which the Russian legation at Tehran derived from it. Russia followed up her loan of 1900 with a further £1 million in 1902. The British sensed that affairs in the Persian capital were slipping beyond their grasp. But would the government at home, or that in India, do anything to remedy the situation?

There were proponents of financial aid even before Russia's success of 1900. Usually it was the Minister at Tehran who favoured the idea. The British government was urged to consider a guarantee for British loans in 1895 and 1898; the political reward, it was suggested, would be out of all proportion to the small financial risk involved.[2] Hardinge,

1   Curzon to Hamilton, 6 September 1899, *Hamilton Papers,* D510/2.
2   Durand to Curzon, 27 July 1898, *Durand Papers,* D727/6.

after 1900, was a strong believer in the idea of financial support. To evade the prohibition about foreign loans which was imposed on Persia by the Russian contract of 1900 he suggested that the British and Indian governments should advance money through the state bank of Persia — the Imperial Bank. He had great plans for the Imperial Bank. The British government ought to buy a controlling interest in it, he recommended, and thereafter the Bank's policy could be subordinated entirely to the requirements of British diplomacy. Quite unjustifiably, Hardinge compared his scheme with the Suez Canal project of 1875. Apart from his wilder ideas, however, Hardinge did see what was needed. In return for any money advanced through the Imperial Bank the British and Indian governments should not ask for political concessions nor should they demand security which the Persians might consider to be onerous. The opportunities for exacting political concessions would come in time.

The Indian authorities dissented. The Viceroy wanted certain assurances from Persia as a condition for any loan. First, that the revenues of all the Gulf ports and the province of Seistan should be pledged as loan security. Second, that any change in Persia's tariff regulations should be submitted to the Government of India for approval; third, that no concessions for railways or economic enterprise in the south of Persia should be granted without the prior consent of the British government. On those terms, Hardinge replied, the Shah would never take a British loan. Curzon did not realize 'that we have now reached a point at which, to be able to make a loan to Persia at all, to be able to break the spell of the Russian loan contract, is in itself an advantage worth paying for'. 'We have got to block before we can conquer', he continued, 'to re-establish equality before we can think of ascendancy, to get back into the saddle before we can put the Persian steed at the fence'.[1] In the end Hardinge prevailed. When the British and Indian governments advanced £200,000 through the Imperial Bank of Persia in April 1903 Curzon did not hide his annoyance that his conditions had all been laid aside.

The decision to provide money for the Persian government had not been an easy one. The dispute between Hardinge and the Viceroy was only peripheral to that which existed between government departments in London and between the Foreign Office and the legation at Tehran. The British government was strongly criticised for the way in which it had handled the Persian loan question in the late 1890s. Again Lord Salisbury was the object of general disenchantment, though in respect of financial affairs the Chancellor of the Exchequer, Sir Michael Hicks-

[1] Hardinge to Lansdowne, 3 March 1903, *Lansdowne Papers*, F.O. 800/138.

Beach, was equally at fault. By refusing to guarantee a British loan to Persia in 1899 the government had missed the opportunity to regain the favour of the Shah. Without a guarantee it had proved impossible for the Imperial Bank to raise money in London. 'It is in cases such as these where the Treasury influence and power in this country are so mischievous', Lord George Hamilton at the India Office observed.[1] Hicks-Beach was totally devoid of imagination, he continued, and had no appreciation of the importance which was attached to loans in oriental countries.

Once again Curzon and Hardinge both agreed. But, as they knew full well, the decision to refuse a guarantee was taken by the whole cabinet, and chiefly on the grounds that the alternative would effectively pledge the British government to a policy of endless financial support for Persia. Salisbury and Hicks-Beach had been able to sway the cabinet without undue difficulty; they could support their argument by pointing to the fact that the House of Commons would never approve the use of public funds for a transaction of this sort. All that Salisbury and Hicks-Beach had done was to apply an orthodox principle, and a principle which was dogma at the Treasury. When chancellors had agreed to guarantee foreign loans before it had only been in some great political cause. The loan of 1833 had been to launch the new kingdom of Greece on the path of political stability and economic progress. That of 1855 to Turkey had been to bolster up an ally during a major European war. A Persian loan in 1898-9 was not in this class. By giving its guarantee for a loan to an effete and spendthrift oriental ruler the Treasury would have opened the flood-gates to requests from all British financiers who wished to invest their money in Asia, in Africa, and in Latin America. Hicks-Beach was the embodiment of the tradition of *laissez-faire* in public finance. Only after he had left the Treasury was there any prospect of effective sustenance for Persia from the British government. When change came in 1903 it really was a new departure: but by then it was too late. It was Russia which, in 1900, most benefitted from the fact that the government in London would not undertake any liability for British capital invested abroad.

In the 1890s discussion as to financial help for Persia centred on the attitude of the British government to a formal guarantee. After 1900 the Foreign Office accepted the idea of advancing money to Persia through the agency of the Imperial Bank. The problem now was to persuade the Treasury to approve the idea and to persuade the India Office to contribute a moiety of the sum in question. The old issue of just how far Persia was an Indian as opposed to an imperial

1   Hamilton to Curzon, 1 March 1900, *Hamilton Papers,* C126/2.

responsibility was again in evidence. The Indian authorities were concerned not 'to be exploited by the Foreign Office'.[1] Indian officials in the early 1900s were wary of advancing money through the Imperial Bank of Persia and doubtful whether loans to the Shah were a legitimate use of Indian revenues. Above all they questioned the effectiveness of financial assistance. An advance could only stave off the country's economic difficulties for a short time. Surely the money would be wasted and the Persian government would then come back for more. Even if the Shah were prepared to mortgage some piece of his territory there were neither the means nor the troops to occupy it in case of default. In 1901 the India Office refused to sanction the use of Indian revenues for Persian loans, and it only changed its view when Lord Salisbury expressed his fear that if Persia turned to Russia again for financial support British influence at Tehran would be totally eclipsed. 'Their refusal to lend the money ought to be put on record', Salisbury advised his staff at one stage, 'in order that the consequences of our having to throw up our influence over Persia may be put on the right shoulders'.[2] Not until April 1903 did the Indian authorities actually participate in a loan to the Persian government. The £200,000 which was advanced by the British and Indian governments through the Imperial Bank on that occasion was supplemented by £100,000 in September 1904. In addition, £½ million was set aside to be used in the future as and when further provision for the Persian government was felt to be necessary.

The question of financial support to Persia, then, proved to be one on which there was considerable disagreement in official circles. From the first serious suggestion of a government guaranteed loan in 1898 until the problem of the Anglo-Indian advances was resolved in 1903, the Cabinet, the Viceroy, and the India Office, each in their turn, frustrated the attempts of the Tehran legation to arrange for British aid. Finance, though, was only one of the issues on which British and Indian officials were divided. The other question to be answered was: how far was Britain prepared to go to maintain the buffer state and to prevent a Russian foothold on the Persian Gulf? Should she not cut her losses and stake out a firm claim simply to those areas which were vital for the defence of India? It was here, as one might expect, that feelings ran most strongly. Everyone, moreover, was involved. Political, diplomatic, and military authorities all had a voice to be heard. Persia was a matter of international prestige, of imperial defence, and of Anglo-Russian relations. The prospect of a great war in Asia loomed

1 Godley to Curzon, 8 November 1901, *Curzon Papers*, F111/150.
2 Salisbury to Lansdowne, 18 October 1901, *Lansdowne Papers*, F.O. 800/137.

always in the background. Truly, the Persian problem was a great debate. Who, then, participated and what were its conclusions?

The chief advocates of change were Lord George Hamilton and his Under-Secretary at the India Office, Sir Arthur Godley. For them Russia's advance towards the Persian Gulf was irresistible. Hamilton set the Persian question in its wider context. Britain had failed to oust Russian influence from Constantinople and to deny Russia control of the Black Sea area. She had failed to keep Russia out of Manchuria and to stop Russia's acquisition of a port on the Pacific coast. Similarly, Britain would fail in any attempt to keep Russian influence out of the Persian Gulf and to prevent a warm water port in the Gulf from coming under Russian control. This was part of Russia's 'natural expansion'.[1] Every year that passed saw Russia stronger in Persia and Britain weaker, and this process, Hamilton forecast in 1899, would continue indefinitely. Certain circumstances favoured Russia's advance. Russia was herself an Asiatic nation. Russian rule was not so alien to those areas of Asia where her influence extended as was that, for instance, of British rule in India. There was no great bar of race within the Russian empire: no inseparable gulf between the rulers and the ruled. Russia could conciliate the peoples over whom she held dominion. The government which she brought, though despotic and at times brutally cruel, was invariably superior to that which had existed before.

Hamilton considered, too, the territorial advantage. Russia was a vast, self-contained, and continuous empire. She possessed great numbers of men readily available for military service in Central Asia. The long land frontier with Persia was, of course, a further asset: Russian diplomacy at Tehran was backed by the threat of invasion. British diplomacy — indeed Britain's entire position in Persia, he felt — rested on the element of bluff. Furthermore Russian diplomacy exceeded the bounds of what the British considered to be acceptable standards. The Russian legation bullied and threatened the Persian government. Russia bribed officials at the Persian court. Her government mobilized state capital for road construction and other financial enterprise in the north of Persia and for loans to the Persian government. All told, Russia would predominate in central Persia in ten or twenty years, Hamilton predicted, and would then establish for herself an outlet in the Gulf. The process was quite irreversible. Changes had occurred in Asia in the closing years of the nineteenth century which operated entirely in Russia's favour and to the detriment of British power.

Godley took up this theme of change and decay in all around him.

1 Godley to Curzon, 15 March 1899, *Curzon Papers,* F111/142.

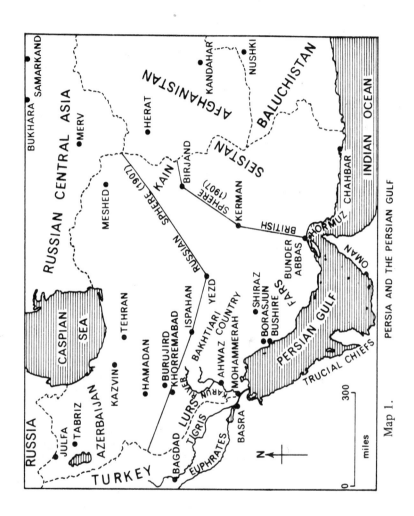

Map 1.   PERSIA AND THE PERSIAN GULF

Godley, like his chief, was a self-confessed pessimist who saw the era of Britain's authority in the world drawing slowly to a close. In the old days Britain's superiority at sea had given her the power to dominate not merely the coastal towns of Asia but also sizable tracts of territory beyond them. Britain's success in the Crimea in the 1850s, for instance, had been largely due to her lines of communication by sea being far superior to those of Russia by land. Now things were quite different. The Russian empire had been given far greater cohesion by a network of railways and her men and materials could be assembled quickly at the scene of any conflict. Britain's control of the seas had diminished in value. It was debatable, in fact, whether Britain could think any longer of waging war with Russia beyond the frontiers of India. Persia had once been almost inaccessible to Russia. Now the Russians were within easy striking distance, and the Russian road system in northern Persia put Tehran, Tabriz, and Meshed completely at their mercy.

Other changes also affected Britain's freedom of action in Persia. European rivalry in the late nineteenth and early twentieth centuries was perhaps the most important of these. By the early 1900s British officials had to reckon not only with Russian aspirations in Persia but with those of Germany and France as well. German ambitions were bound up with the Bagdad railway project. France, in the early 1900s, was trying to establish a foothold in the mouth of the Gulf at Muscat, and her efforts to do so were a restraining factor on the attempts of the British and Indian governments to stop gun-running into southern Persia. In Russia, in France, and in Germany there was strong feeling against England and everything English, Hamilton pointed out. While the Boer War lasted Britain's international position would be extremely weak and nothing should be done to excite the other powers to challenge British authority in any quarter of the globe. Moreover, a war with Russia would in all probability mean war with France as well. The importance of Persia had to be weighed against this wider anxiety. If, by a forceful policy there, Britain drove the powers of Europe to combine against her then the consequences for the British empire might be very serious. Hamilton took the view that Persia and the Persian Gulf were but 'the outer glacis of an extreme bastion, which only in certain contingencies would be necessary for the defence of India'.[1] It was not worth endangering India merely to try to preserve its outermost line of defence.

These, then, were the changes which had occurred — changes in the factors of strategy on a global scale which limited Britain's fighting potential, and changes in the political climate, internationally, which

1   Hamilton to Curzon, 26 January 1900, *Hamilton Papers*, C126/2.

made British officials more circumspect and less inclined to chance their arm. These changes were coupled with the usual restraints on foreign policy which any government in Britain had to face. Parliament was one such restraint. The House of Commons, Hamilton complained, frequently interfered in matters of foreign policy, and even when it did not it was always in the background as a tight financial controller. Then there was 'that foolish and vacillating individual, the man in the street' who also had to be considered.[1] Britain could only take a firm stand on Persia if public opinion were behind the government. If a crisis arose over Persia, no British government could be sure that the nation would be prepared to undergo the hardships and expense which a great war with Russia would entail — particularly not after the years of struggle in South Africa. It was a regrettable fact, Hamilton concluded, that Britain had neither the ability to occupy the south of Persia nor to prevent its gradual absorption by Russia. But it was better to accept that fact than to make pretentious noises at the diplomatic level and then to have to back down with a great loss of prestige when action was required. The home government had no forces available for service in Persia, and the army in India, as far as Hamilton could see, was barely adequate to defend its own frontiers. Nor could Britain rely exclusively upon her naval strength for the defence of her position in Persia. The navy was already stretched to protect lines of commerce and communication all over the world, and if in the future a battle for naval supremacy on the high seas had to be fought the Admiralty could not keep a squadron permanently in the Persian Gulf.

The changes which the India Office proposed were tantamount to a partition of Persia between Britain and Russia. The argument was perfectly logical: it was better to grab what was essential in Persia while there was still time than to risk Russia extending her influence and her control right down to the frontier of British Baluchistan. Arthur Hardinge, at Tehran, was not unsympathetic. Clearly the 'buffer state' was being eroded before his very eyes and the British government either would or could do nothing about it. Hamilton intensified his campaign after Russia's success with the loan to Persia in March 1900. The increase in Russia's hold over the Persian government which would result opened a new phase in Persian affairs. 'Instead of putting forward somewhat nebulous claims in support of the independence of Persia as a whole', he insisted, 'we should now rather concentrate our attention upon those parts of Persia which we consider necessary, either for the protection of India or of our commerce and political

1 Godley to Curzon, 9 April 1900, *Curzon Papers*, F111/145.

interests in the Gulf'.[1] What did it matter if Russia reached the northern end of the Gulf and if she fortified a port? As long as Britain controlled the coastline east of Bunder Abbas, and thereby controlled the outlet into the Indian Ocean, Russian warships could always be bottled-up and her position exposed to attack by superior British naval forces. Moreover Persia's independence was fast becoming a threat, not an asset, to the security of the Indian frontier. While Persia remained an independent state Russia might be able to extend her influence throughout the country. If it were partitioned, however, Russia's control would stop short at the boundary of the British sphere. 'The very independence which we struggle to maintain may become the most effective instrument which Russia can use against us' Hamilton concluded.[2]

There was something novel about Hamilton's suggestion for an Anglo-Russian understanding. It was one solution to the Persian problem. Admittedly the legation at Tehran had suggested co-operation with Russia for the regeneration of Persia in the mid 1890s, but that had not involved such far-reaching concessions. Salisbury too was always willing for an Anglo-Russian *entente*. In fact he had negotiated one for the Far East in 1898-9. Britain agreed to respect Russia's special interests in Manchuria and to refrain from applying for economic concessions in that province; Russia gave similar assurances in respect of Britain's position in the Yangtsze Valley.[3] The British government would have welcomed the prospect of joint loans to Persia. Financial co-operation would preserve the status quo there; financial rivalry was damaging to Persia's independence and to Britain's influence at Tehran. But Russia had never shown any inclination for that sort of understanding over Persia. Indeed, why should she? Hamilton asked. Since her objective was an outlet on the Persian Gulf any understanding with Britain which denied her this would mean renouncing that cherished ambition. Russia declined the British government's suggestions for a settlement of the Persian question in the early 1900s. The prospect of an agreement with Russia was not therefore a very realistic one, but it was a corollary to the general argument which Hamilton and Godley at the India Office, and Arthur Hardinge at times in Tehran, were putting forward. They had their own assessment of Britain's standing in the

1   Hamilton to Curzon, 23 March 1900, *Hamilton Papers,* C126/2.

2   India Office to Government of India, 6 July 1900, enclosed in India Office to Foreign Office, 6 September 1900, C.P. [7590].

3   Details of Salisbury's policy in China and his efforts to reach an understanding with Russia can be found in L.K. Young, *British Policy in China 1895-1902* (Oxford, 1970), pp. 91-9; and J.A.S. Grenville, *Lord Salisbury and Foreign Policy* (London, 1970), pp. 136-47.

world and of her strength in Persia. It was an assessment which made change and compromise essential and one also which provoked the most vigorous opposition.

The alternative school of thought was more traditional in outlook. It maintained that Britain still had the capacity to check the expansion of Russian power in Persia and that Russia should be kept away from the Persian Gulf at all costs. There was no need for an Anglo-Russian understanding; British policy should be quite arbitrary, and efforts should continue to hold the country together as an effective buffer state. The traditionalists were led by the Viceroy — Lord Curzon. Few men had stronger views on Persia. Curzon went out to India in 1899 acclaimed as an expert on the Persian problem and his views reflected the supreme self-confidence which was so characteristic of his career. Curzon, at times, fought his campaign almost alone. Even his Council at Calcutta was divided over Persia. He always had the warm support of the consular service in Persia though, and after 1903 of the two new Under-Secretaries at the Foreign Office, Lord Percy and Charles Hardinge. Curzon's contribution to the debate on Persia was unmistakable. Despite the pessimism which emanated from the India Office in London Curzon remained quite irrepressible. One by one he tackled the defeatist arguments which Hamilton and Godley expounded.

Curzon was critical both of official and of public opinion in England. Admittedly the Boer War was a severe blow for national morale but it would not last for ever. Events in South Africa had weakened confidence and judgement at home. British politicians and officials had become despondent and had lost heart and they tended not to bother about Persia and its difficulties. In India Curzon had escaped all this. His mind was free to grapple with the Persian problem and his enthusiasm was unbounded. 'I would undertake in half an hour with the Shah to say a few necessary things to him that would produce a most salutary revolution in Persian policy and in Anglo-Persian relations during the next twenty years', he wrote to Hamilton.[1] He did not accept that British policy in Persia rested upon bluff. Britain could seize and hold the Persian Gulf, he claimed, without the slightest difficulty; her bargaining power both in respect to Persia and to Russia was therefore considerable. Russia would not dare to make a move in Persia if the British government made known that it would respond by seizing all the Gulf ports of any size. This would frustrate Russia's plan for controlling a port in the area, for it was most unlikely that Russia would risk a major war by actually turning out a British occupation force. 'So long as we retain command of the sea, it seems to me that

1   Curzon to Hamilton, 5 April 1900, *Hamilton Papers,* D510/4.

we can always take Persia by the throat and can always prevent the final consummation of Russia's designs'.[1] Yet this knowledge should not lead to complacency. Only a constant watch on Russian agents in Persia could justify any feeling of security.

Because of the duplicity of Russian diplomacy, as he saw it, Curzon ruled out the possibility of a division of Persia into spheres. The British public, when they clamoured for some understanding with Russia, he complained in 1902, knew nothing of just how untrustworthy Russian officials were. The Russian government would always disclaim responsibility for its officials when they obstructed British interests in Persia; secretly, though, it always encouraged them. An agreement with Russia could only be achieved at the price of surrendering the outlying bulwarks of the Indian empire. Russian officials would never settle for an arrangement which drew a limit to their territorial ambitions in Central Asia; or, if they did, it would surely be discarded as soon as they found it to be inconvenient. Britain had been deceived already by Russia's fraudulent diplomacy over the acquisition of the Central Asian Khanates, over the spread of Russian influence in Manchuria, and over the seizure of Port Arthur in 1898. 'With eternal courage, the Russian diplomat comes forward, presents us with time-honoured falsehood, has note taken of it, and smugly retires' Curzon complained.[2] No one but him was alive to Russia's intrigues or to her insatiable appetite for expansion.

Curzon did not see Russia reaching the Persian Gulf as inevitable. As far as he could discover the only thing in favour of allowing Russia a port in the Gulf was that it would give the British navy something to attack in time of war. 'We can keep her out of the Persian Gulf', he boasted in 1899, 'and I say deliberately that we ought to do it, and that we shall be cowards if we do not'.[3] He resented the idea, so widely held in London, that Russia had some sort of right to warm water outlets. Curzon was unmoved by the arguments of the Admiralty in 1902 that a Russian port at the northern end of the Gulf posed little danger. With a railway linking it to Russian territory, and a 'Russianized' belt of territory behind it, a Russian port could become a point for offence. If this happened a powerful British squadron would need to be stationed in the Gulf and in the Indian Ocean, the expense of which would be a great strain on Indian finances. Curzon opposed concessions to Russia in any part of the world: 'each morsel but whets the appetite

---

1   Curzon to Hamilton, 16 January 1902, *Curzon Papers,* F111/161.
2   Curzon to Hamilton, 23 October 1901, *Hamilton Papers,* D510/9.
3   Curzon to Hamilton, 31 October 1899, *Hamilton Papers,* D510/3.

for more, and inflames the passion for a pan-Asiatic dominion'.[1] He had no wish to increase Britain's responsibilities in the Persian Gulf but a firm statement of intent was needed from the British government.

The Persian Gulf had a fascination for Curzon. He seemed extremely sensitive to the passing paramountcy of British trade and shipping in its waters. His spectacular, but pathetic, tour of the Gulf at the end of 1903 seemed as much a feature of that fascination as of his political motive to strengthen British influence along its shores. He noticed with anxiety the appearance of German, French, and Russian traders. 'I cannot see why we should allow these newcomers, who have spent no money in the Gulf, who enjoy no trade there, have no subjects there, possess no immediately contiguous territories, and are drawn there solely by political ambition', he wrote in 1900, 'to erode, fritter away, and little by little destroy, the great body of interests which we have built up there by a century of trade and dominion'.[2] To protect the Gulf he would tolerate no intrusion of Russian influence into the south of Persia. In his view the Persian government should be plainly told that if it went back on either of its pledges not to allow a Russian railway into southern Persia and not to admit any interference by Russia in the administration of the Gulf customs revenues then Britain would occupy one or more of the ports of southern Persia. 'Let us bar the whole of the south, or give up the game', he wrote to Percy at the Foreign Office in 1903.[3] For Curzon the first step was to make Britain's position clear to the Persian government. He criticised the British government in 1900 for not protesting to the Shah about the Russian loan, and also for not trying to persuade the Persian government to cancel the restrictions on its international borrowing powers. The British government should have exacted some measure of compensation from Persia, he remarked. It might have been possible to get a general pledge about keeping foreign influence out of the south, or some recognition from the Shah of Britain's special interests and position there.

Curzon, of course, was the advocate of strong-arm tactics in Persia. His disappointment was therefore acute when all that the British government was prepared to do was to invite the Shah to England and to feast him at the Guildhall as an old friend. 'Oh my God', he lamented to Godley, 'English policy towards Persia throughout this century has been a page of history that makes one alternatively laugh with derision

1 Memorandum by Curzon, 28 October 1901, enclosed in India Office to Foreign Office, 19 March 1902, C.P. [8085].
2 Curzon to Hamilton, 15 February 1900, *Hamilton Papers*, D510/4.
3 Curzon to Percy, 5 March 1903, *Curzon Papers*, F111/162.

and groan with despair'.[1] The procedure which Curzon proposed involved the use of sufficient threats against the Persian government as would force it to hinder the extension of Russian power into the south. Coupled with this, he wanted a protectorate over Bahrein and Kuweit in the Gulf. He very much supported the old idea of preserving Persia as a buffer state. With Siam, Thibet, and Afghanistan it formed a ring of independent states which separated India from Russia; the task of the British government, he believed, was to retain them all intact. But Curzon showed no sign of hope until Lord Lansdowne had fully seized the reins of foreign policy in London. Only then did he feel that his suggestions had any chance of proper consideration.

For all the eloquence and emotion which the Persian debate inspired there were certain realities which had to be faced. By and large, it seemed that Hamilton and Godley had assessed the state of affairs rather better than Curzon and his supporters. Certainly the argument that the British public would have no enthusiasm for a war over Persia was a difficult one to answer. No Liberal government would try to convince the nation of the need for war: no Tory government would be able to. Britain's international position also made a firm stand against Russia in Persia virtually impossible. The troubles in South Africa occupied the attention of British politicians at the turn of the century, and the obvious delight abroad at this imperial disaster made for caution in British foreign policy. Hamilton was quite right in thinking that Britain was widely regarded as a 'grab-all nation'.[2] British politicians were anxious that amicable relations might be maintained with the European powers. Britain could indeed do nothing but compromise in international affairs.

Then there was the weakness of British influence at Tehran itself which had to be considered. However firm the British might resolve to be, Russia undoubtedly had far greater leverage on the Persian government and could counter the pressure of the British legation without much effort. As long as the Shah and his ministers lived in fear of Russia British representations were often of little more than academic interest. The shortage of money was another limiting factor. In 1901 Curzon was told that money was needed for Britain's extensive commitments all over Africa and that nothing could be expected from the Treasury for Persian affairs. The Boer War meant that £200 million had to be found — one penny on income tax in perpetuity, Salisbury complained. Any war on Persian territory would require increases of two or three times that amount, he continued, and this would be quite

1   Curzon to Godley, 15 March 1900, *Curzon Papers*, F111/159.
2   Hamilton to Curzon, 14 December 1899, *Hamilton Papers*, C126/1.

unpalatable at home.[1] These were some of the hard realities of Britain's position in the early 1900s. They reinforced the case for a change in Persian policy. On top of that there were a number of purely military considerations which affected Britain's capability to counter any move which Russia might make.

By mid 1901 nearly 400,000 men were serving in South Africa. The British government was near the end of its recruiting capacity, and the army in India had been depleted to an extent which left it barely fit for the task of frontier defence. Military and naval reports clearly indicated that operations in southern Persia were out of the question. This was, as Godley remarked, 'a pitiable confession of weakness' for a great imperial power.[2]   In any war with Russia in Central Asia Britain's military resources would be greatly inferior. Moreover, if a line was drawn across Persia which Britain had to defend then that meagre supply of men would be spread out along a far longer frontier than would be the case if they were simply holding the passes on the north-west frontier of India. A Russian naval port in the Gulf, admittedly, could threaten Britain's sea communications and might delay the transport of reinforcements from home to India or the East at a critical time.   So long as Britain held the mouth of the Gulf, however, and particularly the port of Bunder Abbas, the threat from any Russian port to the west of it was minimal. The British navy could seal off the Gulf by a squadron of destroyers, torpedo-boats, and submarines and stop the passage of Russian warships into the Indian Ocean.[3]

Obviously the British government would only contemplate military action in Persia in response to a threat from Russia. The principle, as the Prime Minister explained in 1902, was that 'until Russia moves we remain still; as soon as Russia moves in the north, we move in the south'.[4] Two possibilities had to be considered. First, what should Britain do in the event of war with Russia? Secondly, what should she do if Russia occupied the north of Persia on the pretext of quelling local disturbances? A conference of representatives from the Foreign Office, the India Office, the War Office, and the Admiralty met in November 1902 to discuss these points. In the case of a major war with Russia it was decided that Britain could occupy Seistan and seize

1   Cranborne to Curzon, 29 September 1901, *Curzon Papers,* F111/179; and Salisbury to Curzon, August 1900, *Curzon Papers,* F111/222.

2   Godley to Curzon, 21 November 1902, *Curzon Papers,* F111/161.

3   Memorandum by Balfour, 22 April 1904, I.O. C.I.D. L/Mil/5/729, 1903-04, no. 46; and War Office memorandum, 9 April 1903, F.O. 60/673.

4   Balfour to Lansdowne, 6 September 1902, printed with Hardinge to Lansdowne, 27 August 1902, F.O. 60/657.

the strategic port of Bunder Abbas along with a few adjoining islands in the Gulf. These measures were strictly related to the needs of Indian defence. In the event simply of a Russian invasion of northern Persia Britain's reply would be similarly restricted. Again it was agreed that Seistan might be occupied and that Bunder Abbas and some islands should be taken. Warships could patrol the Gulf and watch over British interests at the major ports, but no territory inland could be held.[1] These contingency plans were, in a sense, the outcome of the Persian debate.

This reassessment of military potential was accompanied by a reconsideration of political policy. Those who had criticized the British government for complete disinterest in Persia were certainly exaggerating. Britain had gained several assurances from the Persian government in the late 1890s which safeguarded her interests. The pledge of October 1897 that the customs of southern Persia would never be placed under foreign control was an important one. The British legation reminded the Persian government of its existence in 1899 and again in 1900. Similarly, the pledge by the Shah in 1888 promising British concessionaires the right to build a railway from the Gulf to Tehran in the event of Russia constructing railways in the north was highly valued by the Foreign Office. The legation succeeded in obtaining confirmation of it from the Persian government in 1900. Admittedly pledges by the Persian government would not stop a Russian army marching to the Gulf if it decided to do so. But by preventing Russian control of the customs revenues of the ports of southern Persia, and by blocking the chances of Russia constructing a railway network throughout Persia, the British government had removed the possibility of a Russian foothold by these means. If the Russian government wanted access to the Gulf it would have to be by force of arms, and Russia might think twice before risking a major war to obtain that goal.

After 1900 there were signs that the government in London was becoming more concerned about Persia. Lord Lansdowne, the new Foreign Secretary, had been Viceroy of India between 1888 and 1894 and perhaps that was one reason why he was more interested in the future of Persia than his predecessor, Salisbury, had been. His tenure at the Foreign Office, from 1900 to 1905, produced marked changes in the course of foreign policy. He was industrious and energetic. Even his political adversaries conceded that he had a sharp mind capable of clear expression; all round, he was an easy man to deal with and an innovator and an admirable co-ordinator in the Foreign Office. Lansdowne acknowledged that things had been allowed to slip in Persia

1 Interdepartmental memorandum, 27 November 1902, F.O. 60/657.

towards the end of Salisbury's régime. He admitted that Britain could not expect to keep the Persian Gulf as a *Mare Clausum;* Britain's monopoly of trade was bound to disappear in time. But he opposed the idea of a Russian naval base in the Gulf and he was not in favour of a division of Persia into spheres. Any partition, he contended, would certainly keep British influence out of the north of Persia but it would not guarantee that Russia stopped her intrigues or renounced her ambitions in the south.[1] Lansdowne realised the need for a clear statement of British interests and intentions in Persia. For that purpose he drew up a long despatch to Hardinge at Tehran, the terms of which Hardinge was to pass on to the Persian government.

Lansdowne reaffirmed that British policy was still to preserve Persia as a buffer state. But this could only be conditional. If the Persian government degenerated into a puppet régime controlled by Russian diplomats, Britain's attitude would need to be reconsidered. Of course, Russian influence was predominant in northern Persia — that had long been recognised. Similarly, though, Britain had commercial and strategic interests in the south which were inalienable, and the Persian government should be aware of that fact. If Persia ceded a naval base to Russia in the Gulf then Britain would retaliate by such measures as were necessary to protect her vital interests. The pledges as to customs control and railway concessions would not be allowed to lapse. The province of Seistan was one to which the British government attached the very greatest importance, and no foreign control would be permitted in the region. Given these safeguards to British interests, Britain would continue working to maintain the integrity of the Shah's domains. Persia should accept British advice and resist the interference of Russia in matters which concerned British interests.[2] Curzon was delighted. Lansdowne had come down on the side of traditional policy and he had explained, in no uncertain terms, the limits of British tolerance. His despatch to Hardinge, sent off early in January 1902, was largely inspired, in fact, by a private letter from Curzon written in the previous June. Lansdowne followed his sharp reminder to the Persian government with a general declaration in the House of Lords in May 1903 which confirmed Britain's determination to prevent any foreign power gaining a naval base on the Gulf waters.[3] The Persian debate was closed. Lansdowne had cast his vote on the side of those who wanted to postpone the day of reckoning.

1 Lansdowne to Curzon, 5 May and 15 August 1901, *Curzon Papers,* F111/149.

2 Lansdowne to Hardinge, 6 January 1902, C.P. [8085].

3 *Hansard* (Lords) 4th ser. CXXI, 1345-8, 5 May 1903.

Hamilton and Godley were not entirely defeated however. The military reports which appeared towards the end of 1902 confirmed their suspicions that Britain had nothing with which to back up her bold pronouncements. Yet Lansdowne had really committed the British government to very little. The tone of his declarations was firm but his threats were very general. Godley, despondent to the last, still believed that diplomatic outbursts were worth no more than the military force which lay behind them. For him, Lansdowne's warning to the Persian government made no difference at all and he wrote to Curzon shortly afterwards that everyone in London had soon fallen back into despair and lethargy about the future of Persia. Lansdowne had taken the bold line, however, in the confidence that a display of firmness and determination by the British government might obviate the need ever to back up its declarations. He was under no illusion about the limited support which he could get from the military authorities.

Curzon regarded this reassessment of Persian policy as 'an immeasurable stride in advance', and one which 'must alway remain a conspicuous landmark of Lansdowne's administration'.[1] The 'buffer state' was reaffirmed and it continued to be the policy of the Tory government until its resignation in December 1905. 'We must continue our efforts to support and, if possible, reform the tottering fabric of the Persian monarchy', the Prime Minister concluded, 'and to retain our due share of influence over the policy of the Shah'.[2] Perhaps British policy rested a little more on bluff than Lansdowne was prepared to concede; but then this outward display of intention was only a part of Lansdowne's grand design for strengthening Britain's position in Persia. Lansdowne's energy for the Persian question led to more than tough pronouncements in the House of Lords and long despatches to Hardinge. As he well knew, these statements of broad policy did very little to consolidate British interests, whether commercial or political, in Persia — and this, ultimately, was what really mattered. The struggle for Persia was not fought with the methods of conventional diplomacy, nor, as it turned out, was it determined by armed conflict. Loans, roads, and local influence — these were the tools with which Russian and British influence in Persia were fashioned, and it was Britain's ability to compete with Russia in respect of these that would decide how effectively the Russian advance through Persia could be halted. Lansdowne and Hardinge were well aware of this, as in fact Salisbury had been, to a lesser extent, before them. They became conscious of the need to transgress estab-

1   Curzon to Hamilton, 9 January 1902, *Hamilton Papers,* D510/10.

2   Memorandum by Balfour, 22 April 1904, I.O. C.I.D. L/Mil/5/729, 1903-04, no. 46.

lished rules of diplomatic and official conduct, above all in the relationship between political policy and private economic interests. Lansdowne had publically restated the nature and importance of Britain's position in Persia, but he had said nothing about his intention to support British interests on the ground. The latter was not a matter for debate but one for quiet and patient effort. Lansdowne knew exactly what he wanted, and, with Hardinge's co-operation at Tehran, he knew also how to get it.

4

BRITISH POLICY 1890-1905

Policy was not just a matter of opinion or debate. It should not be judged therefore solely by general statements of intent made in Parliament nor by the vague expressions of sentiment contained in official or in private correspondence. The debate on Persia ignored important aspects of British policy. The men who had the most to say about Persian affairs were not necessarily those who were the most concerned with, or the most informed of the measures which were actually being taken to defend British interests in the country. Despite the flow of arguments from the India Office and the Government of India the responsibility for decisions lay with Salisbury and later Lansdowne at the Foreign Office and with Hardinge at Tehran. They could never be bold or aggressive: the government had very limited resources at its disposal. The Foreign Office thus devised more subtle ways of trying to restore and to increase Britain's status in Persia, of bolstering the régime at Tehran, and of consolidating Britain's position in the south.

The policy which Lansdowne and Hardinge followed in Persia, and which to a certain extent had its roots back in the 1890s, was highly original in its methods. It did not conform to the general rules of British diplomacy, for the Foreign Office became closely involved with the operations of private finance and the Tehran legation was no longer averse to interfering in Persia's internal politics and court intrigues. The code of conduct which the Foreign Office had laid down was modified to exploit every opportunity. In the 1890s the legation at Tehran showed some signs of what was needed. By the early 1900s the Foreign Office too came to see the need for flexibility in diplomacy.

The nature of Persian society presented certain possibilities. The fact that individual contacts were so important meant that corners could be cut through a judicious use of money and of favours. The invitation to the Shah to visit London in 1902 was part of Lansdowne's attempt to improve relations at the personal level. On threat of resignation, Lansdowne overcame the reluctance of Edward VII to confer the Order of the Garter on the Shah. The vanity of all Persians was such, Hardinge reported, that anything in the way of a personal compliment or a gift made a far better impression than the strongest logic. Gifts could be withheld as well as given. Hardinge warned the Shah in 1903 that the diamond star which was to accompany his award of the Garter would not be sent unless the Persian government proved more pliable in settling the question of the frontier administration in Seistan.

Efforts to win support in Persia were not confined to flattering the Shah. The heir (the Vali Ahd), the governor of the northern province of Azerbaijan, was attended by an English physician in the 1890s who undoubtedly had some control over the political manoeuvres of his patient. In 1895 the British Minister recommended that a special allowance should be paid to keep the doctor at his post. It was important 'to have an Englishman always at the Vali Ahd's elbow'. If the Vali Ahd died before the reigning Shah then the allowance, although perhaps wasted, would not have cost very much. If the heir ascended the throne 'the money will have been well spent'.[1] In fact the Vali Ahd did become Shah after his father's assassination in 1896 and the English physician was retained. The latter was not a great power behind the throne. The Chargé d'affaires was certainly exaggerating when he claimed in 1900 that the physician had a hold over the Shah. Nonetheless, it is quite conceivable that he was 'of immense service to us'.[2] Justifiably, the legation took the view that if the Shah did employ a foreign physician then only good could come from the appointment falling to a British subject.

Less important Persian notables also deserved consideration. The Firman Firma was one of them; he was a member of the royal house, an ex-minister of war, and Governor-General of Arabistan in 1905. The Firman Firma was most anxious that his son should enter a military college in England. Lansdowne wrote to the War Office in August 1905 asking that, for political reasons, the application might be favourably received.[3] At a lower level it was important simply to make a good impression among the population. Hardinge argued strongly that the British consulates in Persia should all have small detachments of Indian soldiers whose smart appearance alone would raise British prestige in the provinces and would counter the influence which Russian agents derived from the presence of Russian Cossacks. The effect of a slight display of strength would be out of all proportion to its actual fighting capacity, Hardinge advised. In the towns of Persia the priesthood, the merchants, local officials, and the general public all drew unfavourable conclusions from the fact that British consulates had no military guards while the Russian ones were well equipped. If the central government had been strong it would not have mattered what the people thought. But the government was weak and it could be easily swayed by the clergy or by public opinion. Lansdowne approved the scheme in May 1901, although the expense, he decided, would have to be borne by the

1 Memorandum by Durand, 27 September 1895, C.P. [6704].
2 Spring-Rice to Barrington, 2 May 1900, *Salisbury Papers*, A/127.
3 Foreign Office to War Office, 12 August 1905, F.O. 60/707.

Government of India. The Foreign Office also retained a military attaché at Tehran 'rather for prestige than because the wretched Persian army is a factor deserving of real study'.[1] Both the Foreign Office and the India Office opposed a suggestion in 1903 that the number of British telegraph officers in central and southern Persia should be reduced: British authority was enhanced by the mere existence of British subjects in those areas.

These measures were minimal, however, compared with Russian tactics, and compared too with the more important aspects of British policy which were intended to manipulate the Persian government. The British legation, quite naturally, was always mindful of which Persian officials were friendly to British interests. It assisted them whenever possible in court intrigues, and it protested against the appointment to high office of Persians who were disposed towards Russia and who were inimical to Britain's cause. Loyalties were quickly made and soon transferred. Sometimes the wrong horse was backed, as was recognised to have been the case in 1890. In the 1880s the British government had supported a younger son of the Shah, the Zil-es-Sultan, who had established himself as an effective ruler in the south of Persia from his seat at Ispahan, and who appreciated the need for widespread reforms and for economic development in the south. In 1888 he fell from power. The Foreign Office realized that 'our so-called ally is played out, and our support of him should go no further than is necessary to avoid the imputation of having deserted him'.[2] That the legation was alive to the importance of helping those who rendered some service to British interests was also evident by its efforts to keep the then pro-British Amin-es-Sultan in power as Prime Minister in 1891.

The capacity of the legation to intercede in court politics on behalf of its friends was an important determinant of British influence at Tehran. It could also make a powerful impression upon those officials who still had to choose between allegiance to either British or Russian diplomacy. The legation could not maintain its standing at court, though, without the necessary support from home. It lost a good friend in the person of the Persian Prime Minister in 1898 after the Shah had dismissed him for failing to negotiate a loan from British sources. His successor in office was widely regarded as a tool of Russian diplomacy; indeed it was he who contracted the Russian loan of March 1900 on such onerous terms. The British paid the price for not keeping their

1 Hardinge to Lansdowne, 1 September 1902, *Lansdowne Papers*, F.O. 800/137.

2 Memorandum by Currie, 13 May 1890, F.O. 60/517. Greaves gives a good account of Britain's relations with the Zil-es-Sultan in *Persia and the Defence of India* pp. 150-5.

friends in high places in Tehran; but the inevitable difficulty was that the men in London could never fully appreciate the importance of doing so. The legation was often making bricks without straw in trying to defend British sympathisers in the Persian government. The Russians could bribe and threaten with impunity, and they usually ensured that the Shah and those around him were deaf to the diplomatic representations of the British Minister.

The picture in the provinces was much the same. The legation tried to establish good relations with local officials but with varying degrees of success. The governors of the northern provinces lived in the shadows of Russian consuls and under the threat of Russian Cossacks. In some cases they were more or less appointed according to their suitability in the eyes of the Russian legation. The British, meanwhile, looked on in envy. The consul at Ispahan considered that the nomination of Persian governors to all seven of the southern provinces should be in the hands of the British Minister and that no-one who was hostile to British interests should be appointed.[1] This was impossible to enforce. To try to do so would have been to risk a serious rebuff from the Persian government, and it might have led to some reprisal from the Russians. In any case, being pro-British was scarcely enough. It was important that any governor in the southern provinces should be firm in keeping disorder at a minimum and in keeping open the roads which carried British trade. Competence as well as loyalty were required — qualities which, the British complained, were hard to find in Persia. The governors of the southern provinces were often men whom the legation would have gladly seen removed. Seldom, however, was it in a position to force the issue at a diplomatic level. Only when it came to Seistan was the British government and the legation resolved to press strongly for their candidate.

Seistan, in the south-east, was of such strategic value that the British could only tolerate a governor who was opposed to the spread of Russian power and who was friendly towards their own interests. Lansdowne urged Hardinge to prevent the fall of the governor in 1901. Hardinge was already aware that 'if we let him fall we shall lose our influence in Seistan to Russia'.[2] If he were replaced by a less accommodating man it would greatly hinder the Government of India's attempt to bring the province firmly under British control. The legation intervened on this occasion and made it known that the British government would take a serious view of any arbitrary dismissal. The effect of this warning, though, was shortlived. In 1903 the Persian government was again

1   Preece to Curzon, 27 September 1895, *Curzon Papers*, F111/62.
2   Hardinge to Lansdowne, 22 June 1901, F.O. 60/647.

planning to dismiss the governor of Seistan, and the legation once more lodged a protest and a threat on his behalf. This pattern was repeated in the following year, despite the Shah's assurance that the governor would not be removed. Not until 1905 did the British finally succeed in securing him in office. In 1905 the legation guaranteed two loans of £830 and £900 to the governor by the Imperial Bank of Persia as a means of strengthening him. When the Persian Minister in London objected to the way in which the British legation had interfered in the internal affairs of Persia, Lansdowne sharply replied that the Shah's compliance in this matter would be taken as an indication of his goodwill towards the British government. Without such an indication, Lansdowne continued, H.M.G. might have to reconsider its policy of recognising Persian sovereignty in the province of Seistan.[1]

Seistan was the most important area of Persia in which the British government felt itself obliged to intervene. It also recognised the possibility of increasing its weight with the tribes of the south of Persia. There were two principal tribes: the Bakhtiaris and the Lurs. In both cases the Foreign Office was concerned to establish closer ties with the ruling chieftains. Both were warlike tribes, both lived in mountainous regions of central and southern Persia where the voice of the central government was very weak, and both, perhaps, could be relied upon to resist with some determination any Russian advance. Military reports as to their fighting potential varied greatly. It was most unlikely, of course, that the tribesmen could match a well-drilled Russian army, even if fighting in their own mountain passes. They remained an unknown quantity, but it was better if their allegiance was with the British than against them. Although the tribes only became an important factor in Persian affairs after the beginning of the revolution in 1905, already in the late 1890s and the early 1900s the legation was on the lookout to improve its relations with them through the British consuls in the south, and by means of the British road network which was under construction and the development of British trade. Admittedly these contacts were of a general nature which would yield results only over a period of time. Ideally the Lurs and Bakhtiaris would keep the roads and mule tracks which ran through their regions free from bandits and thus allow the uninterrupted passage of British trade from the Gulf into central and northern Persia.

As early as 1896 the British Minister at Tehran suggested raising Bakhtiari and Lur militias, trained and led by British officers, to protect the arteries of trade in southern Persia. The idea found some sympathy

---

1 Foreign Office memorandum for the Cabinet, 10 March 1905, Cabinet Papers 1900-05, F.O. 899/5.

but no endorsement in London. The Persian government would regard such a move as encouraging the independence of the tribes against its authority and Anglo-Persian relations would be poisoned for many years. Moreover, the Russians would probably make some forceful response in the north. The Foreign Office preferred the idea of giving a subsidy to the Bakhtiari and Lur chiefs which might be used to pay for a local police force, and Lansdowne sanctioned this scheme. In practice, however, nothing was done. Curzon revived the project for British officers in 1903, 'only to be smacked on the head', he reflected.[1] Curzon and Hardinge believed that Russian agents were at work in the Lur and Bakhtiari country trying to win over the chiefs for Russian ambitions. Meanwhile the Foreign Office and the India Office were still corresponding as to where the subsidy should come from.

The ties which the British tried to establish with these tribes and with the Kab Arabs of the Karun Valley were expected to protect Britain's position in the Gulf in the event of a collapse of central administration in Persia. In the chaos which would follow, the friendship of the most powerful chieftains in southern Persia would be inestimable. Anarchy in the south might be averted, Russia would have no pretext for intervention, and the British government would be spared the worry and the expense of occupying the coastal belt to impose law and order. The India Office recognised in 1904 that future action in south-west Persia largely depended upon the extent to which the Bakhtiaris, the Lurs, and the tribes of Arabistan could be 'utilized' and 'strengthened'.[2] The tribes, it was hoped, would be guided largely by the advice of British agents in Persia, and their territories would form a zone of political stability across the southern provinces.

The south, naturally enough, was the principal focus of British attention. Though the legation did its utmost to direct the course of events in Tehran and to protect its allies within the Persian government, Britain's lack of any power base in the north of Persia meant that it could never hope to cancel Russia's hold upon the Shah and his advisers. The British were more successful in the south; obviously they were far stronger there. British influence was not restricted to the southern provinces however. The legation had a special relationship with one very important class within Persian society — the priesthood. The priests (or Mullahs) had considerable power over the population. It was they, for example, who had led the popular agitation which forced the Shah to annul the Tobacco Regie in the early 1890s. In general they were intensely Persian. As a class they opposed the Shah's

1   Curzon to Percy, 23 July 1903, *Curzon Papers*, F111/162.
2   India Office to Foreign Office, 27 January 1904, F.O. 60/690.

policy of accepting foreign loans on stringent conditions and they were deeply suspicious of Russian designs. The Mullahs doubtless regarded the British with little more esteem, but at least they recognised that Britain was opposed to Russia's advance through Persia and that, in this, there existed a common objective.

Apart from the incidents associated with the Tobacco Regie the British had always been on reasonable terms with the Persian clergy. The British Resident at Bagdad was in close touch with the religious centres of Kerbela and Nejef in Turkish Arabia, where he exercised some control by virtue of funds which he administered on behalf of the clerical leaders. In these cities lived the 'Popes of Persian Moham-medanism', as Hardinge described them, whose authority over the Persian Mullahs, both spiritually and politically, was considerable.[1] The legation began its intrigues with the Persian priesthood after February 1902 when efforts were made to try to stir up opposition to the £1 million Russian loan. Hardinge approved a small bribe to the leading Mullah in Tehran and he dropped the hint of more to come if the priesthood was successful in rousing the people. The consul at Ispahan was also allocated money from the secret service fund with which to win over the local clergy.[2]

Hardinge had to be careful. To incite local protests against a Russian loan was one thing, but in the present state of Persia there was a distinct danger of those protests developing into a general movement against the Shah. He needed permission from London before going any further. How far should the legation subsidise the Persian clergy? he asked Lansdowne in August 1902. What should he say to their leaders when they asked for his advice? 'I am doing what I can with the clerical party', he wrote earlier in the year, 'but it is rather a delicate matter to work them without running the risk of transgressing the bounds of diplomatic propriety'.[3] Lansdowne realized this. Certainly the legation should not be mixed up in any movement or intrigue against the Shah, he replied; but there was no reason why 'a moderate sum' might not be spent in establishing closer relations with the Mullahs.[4] Though, as Foreign Secretary, Lansdowne could not actively encourage Hardinge in

1 Hardinge to Lansdowne, 5 August 1903, *Lansdowne Papers,* F.O. 800/138.

2 Kazemzadeh, pp. 389-97 deals with this relationship between the clerical party in Persia and British diplomatic and consular agents. The most compre-hensive study is N.R. Keddie, 'British Policy and the Iranian Opposition 1901-07' *Journal of Modern History* 39 (1967). See also H. Algar, *Religion and State in Iran 1785-1906* (California, 1969), pp. 236-9.

3 Hardinge to Lansdowne, 4 March 1902, *Lansdowne Papers,* F.O. 800/137.

4 Minute by Lansdowne on Hardinge to Lansdowne, 27 August 1902, F.O. 60/657.

his plan, he was not opposed to the use of secret service funds to bribe the Persian priesthood.

Hardinge's efforts to win over the Mullahs in Tehran were reinforced in 1903 when the Government of India decided to send an agent to Kerbela and Nejef to improve British contacts with the religious leaders. The British should make no secret of their counsel in these quarters, Hardinge wrote. The more openly the British worked with Persia's spiritual leaders the greater would be Britain's prestige at Tehran and the more the Shah would fear Britain's capacity to have him excommunicated or even dethroned as a result of public agitation. Hardinge saw the Persian priesthood as the last resort for preventing the Shah from virtually selling his country to Russia by taking another large loan. His attempts to form closer ties with them, however, were not confined to his own bribery and intrigue at Tehran and that by the consul at Ispahan. The legation was authorised to guarantee a loan of nearly £2,000 by the Imperial Bank of Persia to the sacred shrine at Meshed in 1903. This was to improve the standing of the British consul-general with the priesthood at Meshed; it was also to keep the shrine from taking a Russian loan. True, it was a dubious transaction which might involve the British government in some financial loss. However, 'if the money were eventually lost' the Foreign Office decided, 'we could make it good from secret service without having recourse to the Treasury. The political advantages are obvious and the sum is small'.[1] A second guarantee was considered a few months later but eventually rejected. Overall, the legation in 1902-3 had made considerable strides towards improving its relations with the priesthood throughout Persia. The methods were highly irregular, but, in the view of Hardinge and Lansdowne, the situation in Persia was such that a departure from the normal rules of diplomacy was required.

The Meshed loan illustrates more than just the desire which Hardinge and Lansdowne shared to establish contacts with the Persian clergy. It was also a reflection of the way in which they were prepared to use financial resources in Persia for political purposes. In doing this they followed a policy which had been introduced during Salisbury's administration in the 1890s. Contrary to general belief the Foreign Office had tried to arrange a loan of £1¼ million for Persia in 1898-9. Although Salisbury would not permit a government guarantee he did sanction the idea that a letter from the Foreign Office should appear in the loan prospectus to be issued by the Imperial Bank of Persia. This letter

[1] Minute by Hardinge on Hardinge to Lansdowne, 25 August 1903, F.O. 60/ 677.

declared that the employees of the Bank who were charged with the collection of the customs revenues of southern Persia (on which the loan was to be secured) would be 'recognized and protected' by the legation in the performance of their duties, and that the entire loan contract would be 'noted' by the British government as a 'binding engagement' upon the Persian government.[1] The Treasury reluctantly concurred. No doubt officials there were not particularly disappointed when the loan fell through. Certainly in the case of these negotiations the Treasury had proved inflexible in that it did very little to help the Imperial Bank. But then the rules of conduct which the government and Parliament had laid down permitted no formal commitments to private enterprise. Under Salisbury and Hicks-Beach those rules were unlikely to change much. Only after Lansdowne took charge of the Foreign Office in 1900 did politics and finance in Persia really seem to work together, and even then the measures which were taken could not be exposed to public scrutiny. Salisbury's gesture in promising the Imperial Bank a letter of support did not reflect any real willingness to work through the medium of finance. It meant that, for political reasons, the Shah's pecuniary troubles could not be ignored, and that Salisbury had recognised the need to compete with Russia in the matter of loans to the Persian government. After the Russian loan of 1900 the British finally awoke to the fact that political necessity had outgrown their standards of official behaviour. The loans of £200,000 in April 1903 and £100,000 in September 1904 by the British and Indian governments through the Imperial Bank were in marked contrast to the practice of British officials in the 1890s.

With these two loans the British government embarked on a policy of advancing money to Persia. This was significant in the context of the government's role in foreign lending in the nineteenth century. Admittedly the sums in question were not large and half the total was contributed by the Government of India. But the change in principle was an important one. Even on those few occasions when the British government had given its guarantee to overseas loans such procedures had not involved the direct supply of public revenues to a foreign government. The Government of India, perhaps, could offer some precedent. Since 1880 a subsidy of £80,000 per annum (increased to £120,000 in 1893) had been paid to the Amir of Afghanistan in return for the right to conduct the country's foreign relations. That was all however. The supply of funds from the British treasury to a foreign state was indeed an innovation.

This policy was intended not only to boost the standing of the

---

1   Foreign Office to Imperial Bank of Persia, 24 June 1898, F.O. 60/601.

legation at Tehran and to divert Persia from borrowing more money from Russia. It was also to extend Britain's hold on the southern customs revenues. One great attraction of the advances of 1903 and 1904 was that they were secured on the revenues of the Gulf ports. 'It must be borne in mind', the Prime Minister, Balfour, remarked, 'that our chief object is to secure [a] permanent lien on [the] southern customs and predominant influence in southern and eastern Persia'.[1] Britain, of course, reaped little positive benefit from this: the primary consideration was that they should never be hypothecated for a Russian loan since this would give Russia a pretext for interference in the customs administration, should the repayment of such a loan ever be in arrears. 'The main object of our advance is political rather than financial', Lord George Hamilton explained in April 1903.[2] There was no point in lending money to Persia unless by doing so the British and Indian governments blocked the way for Russia. The lien on the Gulf customs was 'the keystone' of British policy in southern Persia and had to be strengthened at every opportunity.[3]

British economic activity in Persia was not confined to government lending. There were private firms operating there and these received help from British diplomacy. The legation did all it could to get hold of economic concessions for British subjects. Hardinge, for example, assisted in the negotiations between the Persian government and W. Knox D'Arcy in 1901 for a concession to work petroleum in Persia. He realised from the beginning that the enterprise might have important political results. The British government quite plainly regarded D'Arcy not only as the holder of a valuable concession but also as a potential lender of British capital to the Persian government. For years British consuls had encouraged the extension of British trade and economic activity. The consul at Kerman, for instance, in 1895, had raised money from British trading firms in an attempt to bring the telegraph line from Ispahan to Kerman under British ownership. In 1902 the interdepartmental conference in London which drew up contingency plans for British naval action in the south of Persia stressed that the extension of the Persian telegraph system under British management would undoubtedly assist the spread of British influence.

The Foreign Office pushed forward British economic interests in Persia in order to prevent the spread of Russian enterprise. Nothing highlighted this more clearly than Hardinge's efforts to block the construction of a Russian oil pipeline from the north of Persia down to

1 Balfour to Hamilton, 8 May 1903, *Hamilton Papers*, mss. eur. F123/63.
2 Hamilton to Curzon, 3 April 1903, *Curzon Papers*, F111/154.
3 Hamilton to Lee-Warner, 1 October 1901, *Lee-Warner Papers*, mss. eur. F92/3.

the Gulf in 1902. The pipeline, in itself, was useless; but its construction would be enough of an excuse for Russia to send into southern Persia surveyors, engineers, and Cossacks to protect them, in preparation either for a bolder military manoeuvre or else the acquisition of an outlet on the Gulf. Russia made the concession a condition for the loan which the Shah wanted in 1902, and only by offering the Shah an advance of £300,000 from D'Arcy was Hardinge able to force the Russian government to drop this particular demand. Hardinge was fully alive to the dangers of allowing Russian economic enterprise to filter down into the south of Persia. The pipeline was an 'aggressive challenge' to British paramountcy there, he advised the Foreign Office, 'and a serious introduction of the thin end of the wedge. If we lose over it the effect on our prestige and influence will be very bad'.[1] Curzon, in India, saw it as 'a crucial point in the struggle'.[2] Lansdowne was equally perturbed; he had already protested to the Russian government. In the end the Russian scheme was defeated by Hardinge's counter offer of a loan. Here was proof indeed that the struggle for Persia depended very largely on the manipulation of financial resources.

This pattern of official encouragement for commerce and finance was also a cardinal feature of the policy of the Government of India in tightening its hold over the province of Seistan. A Russian consul had been sent there in 1898, and his attempts to undermine Britain's limited authority in the province soon caused grave concern both in London and in Calcutta. Curzon also sent an agent into Seistan and for a few years the region was subjected to their respective intrigues. The British legation at Tehran, of course, defended the provincial governor and it successfully resisted all moves to have him replaced. But to retain their position in the province the British really needed to extend their interests on the ground. In 1902 the India Office tried to interest Sir Ernest Cassel, the wealthy London financier, in a project for the development of irrigation works. 'It would be a splendid counter "coup" to the Russian advance', Lord George Hamilton exclaimed, which 'would make British influence supreme in that quarter'.[3] Cassel, however, declined the venture. Nothing, he replied, would induce him to invest his money in Persia. Curzon, though disappointed, could hardly blame him. No one was very keen about investing money in an unknown part of the world. After all, on a map Seistan was only a spot in a vast desert. Cassel's attitude was typical of that of most capitalists at home. If British officials wanted economic development

1   Hardinge to Lansdowne, 4 February 1902, *Lansdowne Papers,* F.O. 800/137.
2   Curzon to Hamilton, 18 February 1902, *Hamilton Papers,* D510/10.
3   Hamilton to Curzon, 16 January 1902, *Curzon Papers,* F111/151.

in Seistan they would have to find the money themselves.

Curzon certainly did want this, and he was prepared to pay for it. His viceroyalty was a period of great activity in Seistan. He was acutely aware of its importance and he was always apprehensive that the Russians might gain a railway concession from the north, via Meshed, into the province. His policy was to open up the overland trade route between Quetta and Seistan via Nushki. In the last two years, he boasted in 1901, the value of Indian trade with Seistan had doubled largely due to his work. Curzon's motives were unmistakable. 'The objects of the Government of India in opening the route to Quetta and pushing the trade have been mainly political', he pointed out. 'It has been their desire not only to create and increase the trade, but by means of the trade to establish beyond a doubt the superior interest of England in those parts of Persia which border on Beluchistan'.[1] Hardinge, at Tehran, only emphasised the commercial aspects of the opening of the Quetta-Nushki-Seistan trade route in his dealings with the Persian government, though privately he too confessed that its value was mainly political. A thriving trade between India and Seistan would be an invaluable argument for insisting that Seistan should never be governed by an authority unfriendly to Indian interests.

Curzon's energy in pushing Indian trade was remarkable. In 1899 the British government leased the land across which the caravan route from Quetta to Nushki was to run, and the Government of India spent money on improvements to the road. Trade was increased by means of official loans to private traders, by an official agent who was appointed to canvass in the markets of the region, and by the provision of special freight rates on the railway system of western India for goods destined for the Persian market. Special customs regulations also favoured goods passing directly from India to Persia. By 1904-5 the value of trade on this route was over three times the value recorded in 1897-8. A British postal service between India and Seistan was instituted in 1903. Moreover, Curzon succeeded in advancing the British railhead from Quetta to Nushki in the face of the traditional opposition which existed to any railway extensions beyond the frontiers of India. By the end of 1902 he had won over the military authorities in London. The interdepartmental conference in November recommended that 'we should steadily prepare for an occupation of Seistan by extending the railway beyond Nushki, and pushing our trade'.[2] By 1905 Curzon had brought

[1] Government of India to Hardinge, 29 May 1901, enclosed in India Office to Foreign Office, 6 July 1901, C.P. [7887].

[2] Interdepartmental memorandum, 27 November 1902, F.O. 60/657; and Foreign Department of the Government of India: Summary of Lord Curzon's

the province within what was generally recognized as Britain's sphere in Persia. When the 1907 Convention with Russia was under negotiation the British government had no difficulty in gaining Russian recognition of Britain's special interests and her predominance there. The policy in Seistan was a conspicuous success. Were British officials to prove equally successful elsewhere in Persia?

Just as the British cultivated their interests in Seistan so they made every effort to increase their stake in south-western Persia by promoting economic enterprise in the region of the Karun River. The legation had always been anxious to improve the conditions for British trade around the Karun, as was evident by its efforts to persuade the Persian government to open the river to foreign trade and navigation before 1888. Now that this was done it seemed possible to supply the markets of south-western and central Persia with British goods, and perhaps even to recapture some of the ground lost to Russia in the markets of the north. This, anyway, was the idea: it was warmly recommended by the interdepartmental conference in London in 1902. Curzon, in 1900, labelled the whole project as the 'Karun enterprise'. The Foreign Office had thought up the scheme and had for years been pressing the Government of India to support it. 'We have always been told', he concluded, that the Karun enterprise 'is to be the nucleus of a permanent British interest, if not an ultimate British occupation'.[1]

British officials faced the usual difficulty, however, that private investors took no interest in Persia. The increase of trade depended entirely on the extent to which the network of communications in the region could be improved, and this was a major financial undertaking. Even to get a British steam ship to run on the Karun as far as Ahwaz, the British government had to pay a subsidy to the Euphrates and Tigris Steam Navigation Company throughout the 1890s. Half of that subsidy was paid, rather reluctantly, by the Government of India. When the Viceroy questioned the wisdom of continuing payment in 1895 the India Office informed him that to withdraw his contribution would force the British steam ship off the river and would herald 'the decay and death of what influence we have left in south Persia'.[2] Faced with political arguments of this nature the Government of India continued to pay but the success of the venture remained limited. The only way to make the 'Karun enterprise' viable was to construct a system of roads radiating from the river which would serve to distribute British goods throughout the surrounding country.

Viceroyalty vol. IV, Persia and the Persian Gulf, part I chapter 3, Seistan 1899-1905. *Curzon Papers*, F111/531.

[1] Curzon to Hamilton, 4 January 1900, *Hamilton Papers*, D510/4.

[2] Hamilton to Elgin, 14 February 1896, *Hamilton Papers*, mss. eur. C125/1.

In the absence of railway development in Persia road construction became unusually important. The value of roads was not just commercial: it was very largely political and strategic. Russia, for instance, enormously increased her military power in the north by constructing the Enzeli-Resht-Kazvin-Tehran road in the late 1890s. In the northeast Russia built a road from her frontier to Meshed. In 1905 the extension in the west from Kazvin to Hamadan was opened. Commercially, these roads enabled Russian goods to undercut British prices in the markets of the region and, it was feared, they would soon drive out British trade altogether. Russia was closing her grip on the north of Persia. By the use of roads the British hoped to do the same in the south. It was essential that road concessions held by British subjects should be developed.

The question remained though: how could British concessionaires complete their schemes when private investment was not forthcoming? In the 1890s British road enterprise in Persia was severely restricted by want of funds. The major concession for a road from Ahwaz (on the Karun River) to Tehran, which had been held by the Imperial Bank of Persia since 1890, progressed very slowly for this reason. When the Bank asked for government assistance the Foreign Office refused. Its appeals for financial aid in 1892, 1893, 1895, and again in 1900 were all couched in terms likely to impress upon the Foreign Office the political significance of the undertaking, but all were unsuccessful. This attitude in London was most exasperating to the officials at the legation in Tehran who saw road construction as the means of salvaging British influence in Persia. British prestige would suffer if the Ahwaz-Tehran scheme had to be dropped. Aware of this, some British agents in Persia took matters into their own hands. The consul at Ispahan, for instance, wrote to the major British trading houses operating in Persia in 1896 to try to raise funds for the Imperial Bank. Upon the success of the road, he explained, depended Britain's growing influence with the Bakhtiari chiefs. To give up the concession would be equivalent to Britain renouncing her position in Persia altogether.[1] It took some time for such ideas to filter through the channels of power in London, but when they did the response was a positive one. After 1897, and after Curzon's appointment as Parliamentary Under-Secretary at the Foreign Office, British officials seemed to take a far keener interest in road enterprise in Persia and in risking money for that purpose.

The road which attracted the attention of the Foreign Office in the late 1890s was the one planned to run from Ahwaz north-eastwards

[1] Preece to Curzon, 30 November 1895, *Curzon Papers*, F111/62; and 25 April 1896, F111/63.

through the rugged Bakhtiari country to Ispahan, including a link to Shuster. The concession to build the road was held by the chiefs of the Bakhtiari tribe; they had gained it from the central government after several representations on their behalf by the British legation. The Bakhtiaris, in turn, had engaged the British firm of Messrs. Lynch & Company (the controlling interest in the Euphrates and Tigris Steam Navigation Company) to construct the road. The Foreign Office wanted this done as quickly as possible. It was naturally distressed when H.F.B. Lynch and the Bakhtiari chiefs began to dispute the terms of the construction contract in 1897. Anxious not to offend the Bakhtiaris in any way, British officials brought pressure to bear on the company to settle the matter immediately. The political importance of the road was stressed: 'when such interests are at stake', the Tehran legation wrote to Lynch, 'a great enterprise should not be allowed to fall to the ground for lack of generous treatment'.[1] There were other indications of just how valuable an asset the British government felt the road would be. The legation itself conducted the negotiations between Lynch and the Bakhtiaris and in the process it acted as the local agent for the firm. For British diplomats to negotiate a contract on behalf of private interests was an unparalleled measure of intervention. The legation shunned the idea that Messrs. Lynch & Co. should send a representative to Tehran. It stated bluntly that its chances of reaching a satisfactory agreement with the Bakhtiaris were much better than those of any commercial agent.[2] At the same time the legation was also trying to arrange for a British company to be floated which would provide a steam ship service on the upper Karun above Ahwaz.

The Imperial Bank of Persia's concession for the Ahwaz-Tehran road was an even more important venture. This road would link the capital with the Persian Gulf; it would enable British and Indian merchandise to be transported rapidly into the northern and central provinces thereby making it more competitive with Russian goods. But the problem of insufficient capital dogged all efforts to complete the scheme. The Imperial Bank of Persia built the northern section from Tehran to Kum in the early 1890s, but when the Foreign Office turned down its appeals for aid between 1892 and 1900 the Bank wrote off the project as ever being profitable. When Lansdowne came to the Foreign Office, however, he seized upon the idea of building British roads. 'If we are to make anything of southern Persia', he wrote, 'the encouragement of roads offers the best chance'.[3] Lansdowne fully agreed with Hardinge

---

1 Hardinge to Lynch, 26 August 1897, F.O. 60/631.

2 Hardinge to Sanderson, 1 February 1898, *Hardinge Papers*, vol. 2.

3 Minute by Lansdowne on Spring-Rice to Salisbury, 17 October 1900, *F.O. 60/661*.

who argued from Tehran that the concession must at all costs remain in British hands. If the Ahwaz-Tehran road concession were allowed to lapse, the latter warned, 'our place may be taken to our serious detriment by our rivals, and a future artery between central Persia and the Gulf pass under their unfriendly control'.[1]

The legation did what it could to further the scheme. It wrote again to the British trading houses in Persia in an attempt to encourage investment in the road. Again its efforts were unsuccessful. It then suggested that the Imperial Bank of Persia should pool its resources with those of Messrs. Lynch & Co. to raise more money — an idea which the Foreign Office warmly approved and passed on to the respective parties. Both Lynch and the Bank 'appreciate the important political interests involved' the Foreign Office was assured in 1901.[2] Lansdowne was confident that progress in the construction of the road would follow. But Lynch and the Bank could not reach agreement. In November 1901 the Bank decided that it could no longer afford to retain the road and that it would have to cut its losses by selling the entire concession back to the Persian government for the meagre sum of £20,000.

The Bank's announcement was a severe embarrassment for the Foreign Office. Officials there could not pretend, though, that the Bank had not given ample warning. The directors of the Bank had always complained that the project was unprofitable. They claimed that the Bank had only taken it up in 1890 at the instance of the Tehran legation, and they could point to their frequent appeals for aid in the past. Not only was the road unfinished, but there could be little doubt that the Persian government would resell the concession to Russian contractors and that in a short space of time the Russians would complete the road right down to Ahwaz. Hardinge urged that the sale of the road by the Imperial Bank should be stopped. 'The building of this road by an English firm is an important obstacle to Russian expansion south', he insisted.[3] Lansdowne, too, was well aware of the danger. He had a long interview with the manager of the Bank, he 'endeavoured to appeal to his patriotism', and, finally, he persuaded the Bank's directors not to sell the concession for the time being.[4] But Lansdowne could scarcely expect the Bank to retain a concession which was a constant drain on its finances. If he wished to prevent the sale of the road back to the Persian government then it was

1 Hardinge to Lansdowne, 4 March 1901, C.P. [7730].
2 Mackenzie to Bertie, 28 October 1901, F.O. 60/661.
3 Hardinge to Lansdowne, 15 November 1901, F.O. 60/638.
4 Lansdowne to Hardinge, 7 December 1901, *Lansdowne Papers,* F.O. 800/137.

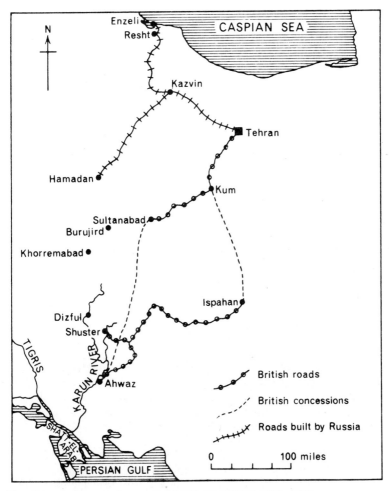

Map 2. BRITISH AND RUSSIAN ROADS IN PERSIA 1890−1907

clear that the Foreign Office itself would have to help the Bank in developing the project. Lansdowne tried again, therefore, to arrange for co-operation between the Bank and Messrs. Lynch; but this time he accepted the fact that some expenditure of public money would be necessary. The Foreign Office offered to increase the Karun River navigation subsidy to £1,500 per annum if Lynch would bring his Euphrates and Tigris Steam Navigation Company into a new company to be formed with the Imperial Bank of Persia for the purpose of road construction.

This was done. The Bank and the Euphrates and Tigris Steam Navigation Company agreed in March 1902 to put up a total capital of £100,000 to found the Persian Transport Company. Negotiations actually to do so were long and complicated. Shares in the Persian Transport Company were not issued until two years later. It was a private company which the Euphrates and Tigris Steam Navigation Company easily dominated by ownership of three times the stock held by the Imperial Bank. In 1902 the Foreign Office agreed that in addition to the increase in the Karun River subsidy the new company would receive a special subsidy of £500 per annum for five years from the British government. Lansdowne had great faith in his scheme; he confided in Curzon that the use of a little money would produce great results in the matter of road construction. But he was quite wrong in this. Lynch thought that the sums in question were derisory, and he began to quarrel with the Imperial Bank of Persia over the terms of their agreement to form the Persian Transport Company. The Foreign Office pressed Lynch to settle quickly with the Bank, but Lynch claimed that the terms which the Bank was offering were so unfavourable as to make the amalgamation impossible. Lansdowne offered a further £2,000. Lynch replied that this was still inadequate and that he would only join in the Persian Transport Company if H.M.G. promised a total of £20,000 for road construction. Lansdowne reluctantly agreed. It was a case of paying what Lynch asked or else giving up all hope of building a British road through central Persia.

The money for Persian roads, like that for bribing the Mullahs in Tehran and Ispahan, came mostly from secret service funds. Lansdowne knew he could get nothing from the Treasury for financing road construction overseas. Sir Arthur Godley, at the India Office, wrote to the Viceroy in December 1901 that although the Foreign Office considered the construction of the Ahwaz-Tehran road to be 'the parting of the ways' as far as British influence in Persia was concerned, 'they dare not ask the Chancellor of the Exchequer for a single penny, and propose to find the whole from secret service money'. This was the only source from which Lansdowne could draw without questions being asked. 'I have not hesitated to use secret service money', he wrote to Curzon, 'and therefore say as little as I can about them [the sums]'.[1] For the original £500 subsidy to the Persian Transport Company and the £1,500 subsidy for the Karun navigation service he managed to enlist some help from the Government of India. Lord George Hamilton agreed to pay half the cost involved, though he felt it necessary to do so without consulting his Council in London. 'I shall have some trouble', he confessed, 'but I do not think they will like to throw me over for so small and at the same time so important a matter'.[2]

So far, Lansdowne had managed the business very well. He had scraped sufficient sums together; but he still had to get Lynch and the Imperial Bank of Persia to sign a final contract for building the road. Instead in 1903 Lynch brought a legal action against the Bank. Lansdowne once again pointed to the political importance of the road and he urged the parties to submit their differences to arbitration. His own position, however, was rather compromised. The Imperial Bank wanted Lansdowne to force Lynch to waive his action. In insisting on this, an Under-Secretary at the Foreign Office realised, its directors were "counting on the objections which we would probably raise to the case being tried in Court and to the source of our contribution being revealed". In public Lansdowne might be thought to have behaved improperly in offering assistance from secret service funds to a private road company. Certainly the Foreign Office feared that any disclosure would be highly inconvenient and would provoke adverse comment in the press and in Parliament. Lansdowne, however, could not force Lynch to drop his legal action. All he could do was to offer Lynch a sufficient amount to sooth his discontent, and this he did at the end of 1903 when the Foreign Office paid out a further £2,000. 'It is worth another £2,000 to get the business through', the Permanent Under-Secretary decided.[3] Lansdowne, who had already committed the government to spending an increasing amount of money on the road, could do nothing but agree.

The Persian Transport Company, which was finally launched in April 1904, was thus the brainchild of the Foreign Office. Hardinge described it as 'our man of straw' in Persia.[4] It was, of course, part of

1 Godley to Curzon, 13 December 1901, *Curzon Papers*, F111/150; and Lansdowne to Curzon, 16 February 1902, *Curzon Papers*, F111/151.

2 Hamilton to Curzon, 2 April 1902, *Hamilton Papers*, C126/4.

3 Memorandum by Hardinge, 5 December 1903, and minute by Sanderson, F.O. 60/678.

4 Hardinge to Lansdowne, 1 July 1904, F.O. 60/714.

the project which Curzon had dubbed the 'Karun enterprise'. But the Company was not very successful. The Ahwaz-Tehran road was still not finished when the British divided Persia into spheres of influence with the Russian government in 1907, and on that occasion the northern half of the road was absorbed into the Russian zone. It was ironic that after so much effort to get the Company off the ground for the specific purpose of countering the spread of Russian power the British government should then have abandoned to Russia much of the area through which the road was to pass by the terms of a diplomatic convention. Such were the requirements of international politics. All the same, the British government's encouragement for road construction between 1897 and 1904, and its subsidy for the Karun navigation after 1888, represented a vigorous policy to consolidate its position in southwestern Persia and to extend trade and communications as far north as possible. It was a striking illustration of the lengths to which the Foreign Office was now prepared to go in supporting economic enterprise for political ends.

A further example of this was the government's aid for the Imperial Bank of Persia as the leading representative of British finance. The Bank operated throughout the country and its strength and stability were bound to reflect on Britain's political status. The Foreign Office had always appreciated the value of a powerful British bank in Persia. The British government had granted the Imperial Bank a Royal Charter at its foundation in 1889 to facilitate public subscription and the legation at Tehran had watched over its interests ever since.

However, the Bank was never very successful. There was insufficient business in Persia for both the Imperial Bank and its principal rival, the Russian Banque des Prêts. The latter, moreover, was virtually an offshoot of the Russian treasury and it was backed by the weight of Russian diplomacy. Intrigues were always afoot, sponsored by the Russian legation, to force the British bank out of business. Hardinge recognized that danger. 'The withdrawal of the Imperial Bank of Persia would be a serious blow to British interests in this country', he wrote from Tehran, 'and to that prestige which is so important a factor in the East'.[1] In the 1890s the legation was sometimes critical of the Bank's management in Persia and it was forthcoming on the issue of staff recruitment with the directors in London. It encouraged the Bank to negotiate with the Persian government in 1898 when there was a chance that the latter would appoint it the sole receiver of revenues throughout the country.[2] The Foreign Office had intervened on the

---

[1] Hardinge to Lansdowne, 30 December 1902, C.P. [8377].

[2] Hardinge to Rabino, 24 January 1898, *Hardinge Papers*, vol. 2.

Bank's behalf in 1894 when the latter applied to the Treasury for alteration to the terms of its charter. Lord Kimberley, the Foreign Secretary, had approved the idea that a private letter should be addressed to the Chancellor of the Exchequer emphasising the political importance of the Bank in Persia and how detrimental to British interests a refusal of the application would be.[1]

After 1900 the Imperial Bank became the agency through which the British government worked when it tried to break Russia's monopoly of lending money to the Persian government. The Foreign Office successfully defended the Bank by protests to the Persian government in 1901, and again in 1903, when the Russian Banque des Prêts was intriguing with Persian officials to gain a monopoly for coining silver in Persia and to undermine the position of the British bank as the sole note issuing agency in the country. The Foreign Office wanted to see a branch of the Bank established in Seistan where it would help to develop the trade between India and eastern Persia which came overland via Nushki. A Seistan branch was not commercially viable, however, and for five years after it was established in 1903 it received an annual subsidy of £1,500 from the Government of India. Again public funds were spent in a most unusual manner to promote financial enterprise.

British activity in Persia was therefore something quite different from the general debate on Britain's strength as a world power and her position in the Persian Gulf in the early 1900s. At one level British officials in London, in Calcutta, and in Tehran differed considerably about Britain's capacity to stem Russia's advance and they were lavish in their criticisms of each other's opinions. At another level they co-operated far more easily in the pursuit of well-defined objectives. Their policy was one of using economic development to confirm Britain's political presence in Persia. Coupled with this, the legation at Tehran was not hesitant in interfering in the country's internal affairs; it fully realised the value of personal contacts and relations and it saw the need for closer ties with the tribes of the south.

Success is difficult to gauge. Hardinge was surely correct in believing that Britain was stronger in Persia by the end of 1903 than she had been in previous years. If the efforts of Lansdowne and Hardinge in the early 1900s are set against the gloomy predictions for the extinction of British influence in Persia which had abounded in 1900 then they might indeed be viewed as fruitful. That Britain's diplomatic leverage was stronger was due mainly to the provision of money for the Persian government and to the fact that the financial stranglehold on Persia,

1 Minutes by Sanderson and Kimberley on Imperial Bank of Persia to Foreign Office, 19 July 1894, F.O. 60/563.

which the Russians had imposed in 1900, had been broken. It is less likely that Hardinge's endeavours to improve relations with Persian officials, to influence the appointment of provincial governors, or to convert the Mullahs into British agents really yielded much tangible reward.

Britain's position in the south was more certain because of Curzon's success in Seistan and because of the hold which the Imperial Bank of Persia had gained over the revenues of the Gulf ports. These measures, in the end, proved more important than the lengthy efforts to stimulate road construction or the 'Karun enterprise' in general. Nonetheless the value of British trade in the Karun region did increase significantly from £16,000 in 1891 to £271,732 in 1902 and the Bakhtiari road was opened to trade in 1900. Overall, of course, there was still no question that Russia remained the dominant power in Persia: but the fact that the total subjugation of the Persian government to Russian diplomacy had been averted, and that the Russians still had not reached the Persian Gulf or overrun Seistan by 1905, said something for the efforts which Lansdowne, Hardinge, and Curzon had made. Their methods were unorthodox, imaginative, and opportunist; they represented a definite break with the past. What they gained, in fact, was time. In the early 1900s the British were able to strengthen themselves in the south of Persia and the government at Tehran was able to struggle on with at least the facade of independence. It was just time enough to allow events elsewhere to run their course — events which took place far away at Port Arthur, at Mukden, and in the Straits of Tsushima.

5

REVOLUTION AND THE RUSSIAN ENTENTE

No one could have foreseen the developments in the Far East in 1904-5. Perhaps a war between Russia and Japan had been predictable but the outcome was a total surprise. British officials could scarcely hide their delight. Their new-found ally had humbled Russia and had shaken Russian power throughout Asia. At home the Tsar was pressed to save his throne. Amid a turmoil of strikes, demonstrations, and riots the Russian empire seemed on the verge of dissolution and about to disappear as a factor in the politics of Europe. The advance in Central Asia was temporarily halted. Persia gained a respite as her people celebrated the news of each Russian disaster. Now it was Russia's turn to take stock of her position and to decide what was possible in Persia just as the British had been forced to do on account of the Boer War. Suddenly Russia needed friends. The British government's suggestion for an accord about Central Asia no longer fell upon deaf ears.

Officials in London and in Calcutta had been debating the merits and the drawbacks of a possible agreement with Russia for several years. Salisbury's policy in the 1890s had been to improve relations with Russia; he saw in this the best chance, as he put it, to maintain an equilibrium in Europe. But Russia had declined British overtures for co-operation in a joint loan to Persia in 1899 and 1901 and failed to respond to the offer of discussions about Persia made by the Foreign Office in 1903. Russian policy in Persia remained quite arbitrary until the Russo-Japanese War. Only in October 1905 did the Tsar express his willingness to come to an understanding with the British government, and even then it was almost two years before the Convention was finally signed. In the interim Russia recovered her position in Persia. A Russian consul was appointed in the Persian Gulf at Bunder Abbas and Russian agents were sent to Burujird and into Seistan. When the agreement was concluded there must have been doubts whether Russia still needed to compromise at all. By 1907, and in the years which followed, it was principally fear of German interference in Persia which drove the Russian government to work with Britain.

The Convention of 31 August 1907 was more than simply a settlement of the Persian problem. This was not just because Afghanistan and Thibet were included, but because it marked a new direction in British foreign policy.[1] Thereafter it was one of Britain's chief concerns

1 The Convention is more fully dealt with in Churchill, *Anglo-Russian Convention*. A briefer, but more recent, study is I Klein, 'The Anglo-Russian Convention

to give no offence to Russia and to keep alive the spirit of co-operation. Both powers declared their respect for Persia's independence. Both expressed the wish for order to be preserved, for peaceful economic development, and for equal opportunities for the trade of all nations throughout the country. Persia was divided into zones of influence — Russian in the north and British in the south-east. Each power agreed not to support its subjects in obtaining economic concessions in the other's sphere. Between the two spheres was a neutral zone in which both powers undertook not to oppose concessions to the other.

The Convention, on the British side, was the work of three men: Sir Edward Grey, the Foreign Secretary after December 1905, his Permanent Under-Secretary until 1910, Sir Charles Hardinge, and the Ambassador at St Petersburg from 1905 to 1910, Sir Arthur Nicolson.[1] All three held out great hopes for the future. In Nicolson's opinion the Convention would give Britain 15 or 20 years of peace and a breathing space in the world arena and it would provide a political framework in which the peaceful regeneration of Persia might occur. Grey thought the terms of the Convention were most advantageous. Britain gained strategically by limiting Russia's zone to the northern provinces since that region was *de facto* under Russian influence already. In ten years time a combination of Britain, Russia, and France might be able to control the course of events in the Near East, he continued. The French Ambassador, in the style of true diplomacy, congratulated Grey on his achievement in September 1907 by pointing out how Britain had obtained Russia's recognition of British predominance in Seistan and over a large stretch of the littoral of southern Persia while, in return, simply acknowledging Russian influence over vast tracts of mountain and desert in the north.

Yet for all these congratulations the 1907 agreement was in some ways an admission of weakness by the British government. Only by

and the Problem of Central Asia 1907-14' *Journal of British Studies* II (1971). More specific to British and Russian policies in Persia are R.L. Greaves, 'Some Aspects of the Anglo-Russian Convention and its Working in Persia 1907-14 I and II', *Bulletin of the School of Oriental and African Studies* 31 (1968). A substantial survey of Anglo-Russian diplomacy in Persia during the period of the Convention of 1907 is to be found in Kazemzadeh, pp. 448-679.

1 Charles Hardinge was a cousin of Sir Arthur Hardinge. All subsequent references are to Charles Hardinge unless otherwise stated. Hardinge became Viceroy of India in 1910 and remained in India until 1916. He was raised to the peerage as Lord Hardinge of Penshurst, but, for the sake of consistency, I have referred to him as Charles Hardinge throughout. All references to the Hardinge Papers are to those of Charles Hardinge. These are preserved in the University Library, Cambridge, save for a small collection which is at the Public Record Office in London. Nicolson replaced Charles Hardinge as Permanent Under-Secretary at the Foreign Office in 1910. He remained at that post until 1916.

recognizing Russian dominance in the north could the central and southern provinces be preserved as fields for British economic enterprise and as a belt of neutral territory to protect her position in the Persian Gulf. This was the value of the arrangement in British eyes. It was, in effect, an attempt to buy off the Russians by abandoning all pretentions to political influence in northern Persia and by allowing Russia the privilege of exclusive economic development there. The Anglo-Russian Convention was the logical corollary to the debate on Britain's military and naval strength in Persia which had been resolved some years before, since it accepted the fact that the 'buffer state' could only be maintained with the collaboration and the self denial of the Russian government. Old Sir Thomas Sanderson, who had served as Permanent Under-Secretary at the Foreign Office under both Salisbury and Lansdowne, acknowledged that the 1907 Convention was the best that could be done in the circumstances. 'We could not pursue a really successful policy of antagonism to Russia', he reflected, 'without efforts and sacrifices which the public and Parliament would not agree to'.[1] Both Britain and Russia entered the contract over Persia conscious of their respective weaknesses in the region. The difference was that Russia's weakness was a passing consideration whereas that of the British was much in evidence right up to 1914. It remained to be seen whether an agreement born under such circumstances could survive the strains which were created when the principal partner recovered both its strength and its desire for independent action.

The pact with Russia never lacked its critics. Curzon, in the early 1900s, had argued strongly against any such bargain. The Indian authorities, both in London and in Calcutta, shared his views. They thought that the Foreign Office had compromised the security of the north-west frontier of India by making any concession at all to Russian expansion. In a country such as Persia spheres of influence could soon become protectorates; the Russians would not miss the opportunity to occupy the entire region up to the frontier of the British zone. The Indian army would then be forced to occupy Seistan to keep the Russians out and the military authorities would be left to defend an advanced line with resources which were hopelessly inadequate.[2] The Convention, in fact, had been pushed through over the head of the Government of India and scant regard had been paid to the reports of the Indian High Command.

The Minister and nearly all his staff at Tehran were also opponents

1 Sanderson to Spring-Rice, 6 August 1907, *Spring-Rice Papers,* F.O. 800/241.
2 Memorandum by Fitzpatrick, 12 June 1906, I.O. L/P&S/10/122, 1907, file: 3128.

of the 1907 arrangement. Russia merely wanted a truce, they argued. Her statesmen would accept no shackles on their freedom of action in Central Asia once Russia was again strong enough to press forward towards the coveted goal of an outlet on the Persian Gulf. Lord Percy, who had been Lansdowne's deputy in the Tory government, also spoke out strongly against the Russian agreement. Like Curzon he believed that Russia could never be trusted to honour any commitment which she had given in a moment of weakness. Others were annoyed that the British zone was so small and that it did not include south-west Persia, around the Karun, which was the main area of British commercial enterprise. Grey, Nicolson, and Charles Hardinge rebuffed such narrow-minded observations. The Convention, they claimed, should be set in the context of improved Anglo-Russian relations in Europe and throughout the world. The Government of India was acting disloyally in grumbling. The Viceroy was bluntly told in 1906 to 'drop the old fixed superstitions' and to accept the fact that 'the international wind has changed its quarter for good or for evil'.[1] Curzon, by 1912, apparently still had 'not shaken off the prejudices and traditions of pre-Convention days'.[2] To Curzon's mind the agreement with Russia surrendered all that the British government had been fighting for over the past century and it gained nothing in return. Grey spent the next seven years defending his policy of co-operation with Russia from a barrage of protest in Parliament, particularly with regard to Russian activity in Persia.

The Convention with Russia was always at the forefront of British policy in Persia after 1907. However much the Indian authorities disliked it, and however fierce the rebukes in Parliament, the Foreign Office clung to its belief that a good understanding with Russia was the overriding consideration. Had Persia held together the Convention might have worked more smoothly. The British government might have been spared the embarrassment of following a policy which, at times, seemed to have neither rhyme nor reason. But Persia did not hold together. The decaying structure over which the Shahs had ruled in the nineteenth century at last began to crumble in 1905, and in the hierarchy of nations Persia passed from the ranks of the sick to those of the dying. Discontent was rife in Persia by the mid 1900s. The extravagence of the Shah and his foreign travels made a bad impression. The Persian government seemed to be under foreign control: it borrowed heavily abroad on onerous terms, the customs service was supervised by a Belgian official, and the economic exploitation of the country was

---

1 Morley to Minto, 11 April 1906, *Morley Papers,* mss. eur. D573/1.
2 Nicolson to Buchanan, 30 July 1912, *Nicolson Papers,* F.O. 800/358.

largely in the hands of foreign concessionaires. On top of that the régime was brutal and oppresive. The Shah kept his throne (and the Prime Minister his office) only by the instrument of terror which stifled for a time the anger and the anguish of his people. In December 1905 the protest came out into the open when a number of merchants and Mullahs took refuge in a Tehran mosque and demanded political reforms. The government managed to brush aside this incident with empty promises but the movement for reform in Persia grew rapidly thereafter. In July 1906 over 10,000 Persians took sanctuary in the grounds of the British legation and refused to leave until the Shah had granted a constitution for the country and agreed to summon an elected assembly (Majlis). On 5 August 1906 the Shah submitted: the constitutionalists had won the first round in the Persian revolution.[1]

After Russia's defeat by Japan and the Anglo-Russian Convention which followed, the growth of Persian nationalism was the second major factor which shaped British policy in Persia in the late 1900s. British observers were conscious of the changes which were underway there. The growth of a spirit of patriotism among the Persian people was in sharp contrast to the lethargy and resignation with which they had accepted foreign domination in the decade before. Persian nationalism was anti-foreign and anti-dynastic. The reform party was against further foreign loans and against the allocation of any more economic concessions to foreign interests. It opposed autocracy, it abhorred the idea of European controllers of Persian revenues, and it hated the agents of the Russian government who had imposed their will over the northern provinces of the country and whose influence was so strong with the Shah and his ministers. A scheme was afoot in 1907 to raise sufficient native capital to establish a national bank for Persia which might free the Persian government from its reliance on the British Imperial Bank of Persia and the Russian Banque des Prêts. All the towns in Persia now had their local assemblies, the British Minister reported, which dispensed their own form of justice and administration independently of the central government. The Shah faced the prospect of strikes and riots throughout the country. The old Prime Minister was assassinated in August 1907. The Majlis got rid of the Belgian customs supervisor in 1907 despite the efforts of the British legation to keep him in office. The Majlis also blocked all attempts by the Shah to get an Anglo-Russian loan. This opposition to all things foreign, whether advice or institutions, would in the end prove harmful to Persia's

1 E.G. Browne, *The Persian Revolution of 1905-09* (Cambridge, 1910) pp. 111-9. This remains the best major work on the Persian revolution. Aspects of the Persian revolution are also covered in A.K.S. Lambton, 'Persian Political Societies 1906-11', *St. Antony's Papers* 16 (London, 1963).

interests, the legation forecast, but to take any steps to thwart the nationalist cause would only make matters worse. The Minister advised that Britain should keep out of the civil disturbances in Persia as much as possible and that she should encourage Russia to do the same. Policy, for the moment, should be to refrain from interfering in the revolution. Events in Persia should be allowed to run their course.

That course was not a smooth one. Although the dying Shah confirmed the constitution in January 1907, his son and successor, Mohammed Ali, never ceased to plot against the Majlis. He retained the loyalty both of the courtier aristocracy in Persia and of the Persian Cossack brigade and its Russian officers. He tried to crush the nationalist movement in Tehran in December 1907 but failed. In June 1908 he tried again and this time, with the help of the Cossack brigade, he temporarily succeeded. Persia erupted into civil war. Royalist troops tried to restore the authority of the central government throughout the country and revolt died down in all the towns of Persia except Tabriz. Without decisive foreign intervention, though, the Shah's cause was always lost. Encouraged by the Turkish revolution of July 1908, the nationalist movement in Persia gradually regained its ground. In July 1909 Mohammed Ali was forced to abdicate when the nationalist armies entered Tehran and his young son was proclaimed Shah as a constitutional monarch. The revolution was over. Now the British waited to see if the new régime could do any better than the old.

British officials had sympathy for the reform movement in Persia. An oppressed people struggling for liberty appealed to their sense of justice — especially if it worked to their advantage. In a sense it did. The constitutionalists in Persia and the intelligentsia of the major towns looked to liberal England for inspiration, just as the Shah and his followers looked towards despotic Russia for the support which they hoped would keep them in power. Inevitably the Persian revolutionaries had the blessing of the bulk of the Liberal party in London, and the more radical members of that party decried any action by the British government which appeared to sacrifice the cause of Persian reform on the altar of the Russian Convention. The Persian nationalists also had friends in the British legation at Tehran, especially the Minister himself — Sir Cecil Spring-Rice.

Spring-Rice had served in Persia before. He had been a member of the legation staff between June 1899 and February 1901 and he had been left in charge for several months pending the arrival of Sir Arthur Hardinge. Now he was being transferred from St Petersburg where, due to his dislike of the Russians, he had been quite out of place. Spring-

Rice hated Persia too, but not the Persian people. He returned to Tehran as Minister in September 1906 and retained his appointment until November 1907. From the outset his feelings were with the movement for reform. He was suspicious of Russian ambitions and, of course, opposed to the 1907 Convention. For that reason his relations with the Foreign Office were often unsatisfactory. In addition, Spring-Rice had poor health and his young wife and child were as great a source of worry to him as was the fate of Persia. 'I wish I were home', he confided soon after his arrival. 'In five years from now I may be having my pension! I am casting about for a side door out'.[1] Spring-Rice was a sorry figure in Tehran. He suffered often from depression and his judgement of events and of the future for British interests in Persia was unduly pessimistic. None the less many of his views were shared by his junior staff. One of the assistants in 1907 considered the Convention an 'infamous conspiracy to crush the liberties of an oppressed people'. 'I should like to be able to leave my service', he reflected, 'and I have qualms as to my right to remain in the service of masters with whom I am in total disagreement'.[2] The radicals at home felt less constrained. For them Russia was the symbol of autocracy whose policy was to back the Shah against the popular party. To co-operate with such a régime was anathema to them. Having foiled the Duma at home, they observed, the Tsar was now determined to help a fellow despot to destroy the Majlis in Persia. Britain, whose prestige in Persia had suddenly become supreme when the reform movement began, had betrayed all those looking to her for guidance and encouragement by signing an agreement with Russia.

The new government in London after December 1905 was something of an unknown quantity. So too was the man who was to hold the post of Foreign Secretary until December 1916 — Sir Edward Grey. Grey remains an enigmatic character. Not unreasonably he has been described as the last Foreign Secretary in the great nineteenth-century tradition.[3] Because of the complexity of the problems with which he had to deal and the dwindling power which Britain could wield in world affairs his position was incomparable with that which his predecessors had enjoyed. By necessity Grey relied more heavily on his permanent staff than

---

[1]   Letters by Spring-Rice, 7 December 1906 and 23 April 1907, in Gwynn, II, 90 and 97.

[2]   Smart to Browne, 12 August 1908 and 10 September 1908, *Browne Papers,* file: letters from Persia 1905-09.

[3]   K. Robbins, *Sir Edward Grey* (London, 1971), p. 372. This is the most recent and most authoritative biography of Grey. It touches from time to time on Grey's policy in Persia, and on Grey's handling of his staff at the Foreign Office. See also Grey's autobiography *Twenty-Five Years 1892-1916* (London, 1925), I, 152-71.

either Salisbury or Lansdowne had done. With Charles Hardinge as his Permanent Under-Secretary Grey ran the Foreign Office smoothly. His relations with Sir Arthur Nicolson, who replaced Hardinge in 1910, were at times less cordial. It would be unfair to speak of Grey as weak, although he often came close to deserving that description. In 1912 even one prominent Liberal referred to his 'ignorance, obstinacy, and plasticity in others' hands'.[1] Lansdowne at one stage had thought that Grey, when coming into office, would simply offer Russia an outlet on the Persian Gulf 'out of sheer good nature'.[2] Certainly the military party in St Petersburg had for many years looked forward to the prospect of a Liberal government in England. Grey was well known for his desire for better Anglo-Russian relations and he might therefore turn out to be more pliable from the Russian point of view. A Liberal government was far less likely to lead the nation into war with Russia over the fate of a backward Asiatic kingdom on the frontiers of India.

Lansdowne had seen Persia as a factor in imperial defence. For Grey, Persia was set more firmly in the context of European politics. Grey saw in 1906 that Russia was weak. Nicolson, in St Petersburg, was uncertain that the Tsar could survive and doubtful that Russia could, for some time, regain her standing as a European power. Grey's policy was to re-establish Russia in the councils of Europe. Without her Germany was too powerful in Central Europe and France would be left to bear the full brunt of German military power. Grey needed an 'eastern front' in the diplomatic struggle. He also needed the potential to be there for an eastern front in case of war. This was the equilibrium in Europe of which Salisbury had written back in the 1890s and which the Russo-Japanese War had practically destroyed. By cultivating good Anglo-Russian relations, and by opening the London money market to the Russian government, Grey hoped to rectify this imbalance. He needed Russia not only strong but friendly also, and he had to be prepared, therefore, to accommodate the wishes of the Russian government in such matters as were important to it. Clearly Persia was one such matter. In fact, Grey's opponents in England, in India, and in the Tehran legation complained that Russia was effectively pursuing her own policy in Persia despite the terms and the spirit of the 1907 Convention.

By 1910 even so firm a believer in the Russian agreement as Charles Hardinge could not conceal his suspicion that Russia was acting contrary

---

1   Stokes to Browne, 30 September 1912, *Browne Papers*, correspondence with C.B. Stokes. The words were those of C.P. Scott, the editor of the Manchester Guardian.

2   Lansdowne to Curzon, 16 February 1902, *Curzon Papers*, F111/151.

to the spirit of co-operation. The Russians had firmly installed themselves at all the points in their zone of influence which were of any
political or strategic importance. The new British Minister in Persia,
Sir George Barclay, noted that the Persian government was subjected
to constant diplomatic pressure from the Russian legation. After the
signing of the 1907 Convention the Russian Minister in Persia was
conspiring with Mohammed Ali Shah against the movement for reform
just as he had been before. Although in public the Russian representative joined his British colleague in urging the Shah to accept a constitution in the interests of law and order, in private he abetted the counter
revolution of June 1908 and he even helped the deposed Shah when the
latter attempted to regain his throne by force in 1911. The Russians
consistently favoured the Shah. Only Grey's representations at St
Petersburg averted more open Russian assistance. The coup of June
1908 was carried out by the Russian Colonel Liakhoff and his Cossack
brigade who went so far as to surround the British legation in order to
prevent the leaders of the nationalist movement from taking refuge
there. 'At present Russian influence is being used in every way possible
to back up the Shah', the British Chargé d'affaires complained at the
time, 'and this is not the non-interference agreed on'. The Russian
Minister 'is sacrificing our good understanding to keep a Shah on the
throne who is in every way worthless', he continued, 'and who may at
any moment be assassinated'.[1]

Even when the Shah's cause was irretrievably lost the Russians still
made trouble for the new régime. In February 1910 Barclay reported
that the Russian legation was giving sanctuary and papers affording
Russian protection to the most disreputable and criminal elements in
Persian society and was thereby weakening the authority of the Persian
government. The Russian government refused to allow the operation of
a Persian gendarmerie with officers of foreign nationality in the northern
provinces. The Cossack brigade, with its Russian officers and military
instructors, was the only force for keeping order which Russia would
tolerate in her zone. This was a great pity the British Minister remarked.
He believed that the Persian gendarmerie had done good work in
quelling disturbances and keeping peace in the south. Russia's policy
appeared to be one of opposition to any measure which might help
Persia to recover. Meanwhile Russian consuls in the north of Persia, in
conjunction with Russian troops which had occupied the region, imposed their own brand of administration. All the consuls were hostile
to British interests as well as to the popular movement for reform, and
they secretly worked for the restoration of the Shah and his autocratic

powers. Their actions were high-handed. The consul at Meshed, for instance, arrested one of the Persian governors in 1913 and entrusted him as prisoner to a force of Russian Cossacks. At Tabriz the Russian consul was able to force the Persian governor to expel the agent of the Tehran government. Sir Walter Townley, who succeeded Barclay as Minister in Persia in 1912, doubted whether Russia desired any improvement in the state of the country at all. Russian consuls frustrated all attempts at financial reorganisation in the northern provinces. They hounded down all those who resisted Russian authority and suppressed all anti-Russian propaganda. The consuls and the military commanders virtually governed the Russian sphere. Persian nationalists were arrested, hanged, or exiled; revolutionary units were disarmed and scattered. If this was the extent of Russian non-intervention, Grey's critics complained, how could the British government continue to co-operate with a power whose aim was simply that of territorial aggrandisement in Central Asia?

The divergence of British and Russian policies was much in evidence over the Russian occupation of northern Persia. Russian troops had massed on the frontier towards the end of 1908 and but for Grey's persistent pleas at St Petersburg not to interfere in the Persian revolution they would have crossed into the northern provinces at once on the pretext of restoring law and order in the Russian sphere. As it was, Russian forces entered Persia in April 1909 when the siege of the nationalist stronghold at Tabriz by royalist forces endangered Russian lives and property in the town and Russian trade throughout the region. Russian troops went on to occupy Kazvin. By the end of 1911 10,000 Russian men were in Persia. By 1914 that figure had doubled. In March 1912 a Russian force bombarded the sacred shrine at Meshed and occupied the city. The Indian authorities were horrified. The Secretary of State in London wrote to Charles Hardinge, now Viceroy of India, that 'the series of events in Meshed seems absolutely inexcusable on any theory, even that of deliberate conquest by Russia'.[1]

The British government had never denied that Russia was entitled to police the territory adjacent to her own frontier.[2] Such intervention, though, was not to lead to any interference in the administration of the country or to take on the appearance of a lasting occupation. Grey appealed to the Russians not to enter Persia and after they had moved in he constantly urged them to withdraw. Britain did not seek to weaken Russia's power in the northern sphere by doing so, Charles

1 Crewe to Hardinge, 15 August 1912, *Hardinge Papers,* vol. 74.
2 Balfour to Lansdowne, 31 March 1905, and Lansdowne to Hardinge, 31 March 1905, F.O. 60/701.

Hardinge wrote to Nicolson: 'all we want is that their action should be in conformity with our agreement and with the principle of the independence and integrity of Persia'.[1] Grey's motives were twofold. Russian control of northern Persia was a breach of the spirit of the Convention. It was incompatible with his desire to uphold the sovereign integrity of Persia and to use the country as a buffer state. Furthermore, from the European viewpoint, Grey did not want to see the Russians dissipating their resources in holding down an area which might be entering a long phase of disturbance and disorder. But for all his efforts, and for all the promises of withdrawal which the Russian government so freely gave, nothing seemed to happen. By the end of 1910 the Foreign Office felt that the movement of Russian troops was placing a serious strain upon the *entente*. In December 1911 the Russians were threatening to occupy Tehran itself. The Ambassador in Russia intimated that neither Grey nor the Liberal government would survive the consequences of such a move and that the 1907 Convention would collapse. Yet not until the middle of 1914 did the Russians pull back the advanced force from Kazvin. By then the myth of Anglo-Russian co-operation in Persia had long been exposed.

Russia's moves to aid the Shah against the constitutionalists, her occupation of the north of Persia, and the arbitrary actions of her agents there provided ample evidence for the Government of India, and for radical opinion in England, that Russian policy worked towards well-defined objectives, independent of the understanding with Britain. So too did Russian intrigues to obtain the dismissal of Morgan Shuster, the American financial adviser who had arrived in Persia at the invitation of the Majlis in May 1911. Shuster set about his task of re-organizing the finances of Persia with considerable ability and enthusiasm, but alas with little tact. Writing three years later he referred candidly to his seven months in Persia as 'my conflict with Sir Edward Grey and the Russian Foreign Office'.[2] He tried to act independently of both Britain and Russia, to bring the entire finances of the country under his own supervision, to obtain a free hand from the Majlis in allocating important railway concessions and in raising foreign loans, and to organise his own gendarmerie. The Russians were wary from the outset. Only Grey's appeal to the Russian government on behalf of the scheme had made it possible at all. By October 1911 the Russian government was determined that Shuster should go. Russian influence at Tehran no longer had the predominance 'to which they considered it to be entitled and on which they mean to insist', the British Chargé

1   Hardinge to Nicolson, 9 June 1909, *Nicolson Papers*, F.O. 800/342.

2   Morgan Shuster to Browne, 14 July 1914, *Browne Papers,* correspondence with Morgan Shuster.

d'affaires wrote from St Petersburg.[1] Shuster's dismissal formed part of the ultimatum which the Russians presented to the Persian government in December 1911 when Russian troops stood poised to occupy the capital. At Russia's instigation a makeshift Persian government got rid of Shuster and dissolved the Majlis on 24 December. Again Russia had intervened to destroy any chance of administrative or financial improvement in Persia.

The critics of the British government could also point to Russia's obstructive tactics when it came to Persian loans. In August 1906 Britain and Russia had agreed to offer money jointly to the Persian government, but in the following year the British legation reported that the Russians were secretly supplying the Shah with funds to enable him to withstand the pressure for constitutional reform. After 1909 Russia no longer showed enthusiasm to advance money, now that a constitutional government was in power, except on conditions which were wholly unacceptable to Persian opinion. Russia's approach was most discouraging, Barclay wrote from Tehran. Her refusal to lend was inexplicable, except on the hypothesis that Russia wished to render government under the new régime impossible. 'This is a reversion to the attitude to which it was hoped that the Anglo-Russian agreement had put an end', an official in London observed, 'and is entirely opposed to the letter and the spirit of that instrument'.[2] Moreover, the Russian government objected very strongly to any proposal by which private British financiers might lend money to Persia until the Persian government arranged for the consolidation of all its debts to Russian institutions. Not only was Russia cutting off Persia's access to foreign capital but she was actually demanding from an empty treasury the repayment of debts.

As judged by her enemies, then, Russia pursued a policy in Persia which served nothing but her lust for conquest. By diplomacy Russia had done everything possible to keep Persia weak and disorganised. By force she had invaded and had imposed her own command over the northern provinces. By intrigue she had done all that she could to sustain an autocratic ruler who was little more than a Russian puppet. At the same time, though, most British observers made few allowances for the difficulties with which the Russian government was faced.

Ostensibly Russian policy was inoffensive. The Russian Foreign Minister, Isvolski, had assured Nicolson in 1907 that he would not interfere in the internal affairs of Persia, that he would take no military

1   O'Beirne to Nicolson, 20 October 1911, *Nicolson Papers*, F.O. 800/351.
2   Minute by Norman on Barclay to Grey, 26 September 1910, F.O. 371/964.

action unless it was absolutely necessary, and that he would always collaborate with the British government. Nicolson sensed no trickery here. Isvolski was an honest advocate of the Anglo-Russian agreement, he declared, whose relations with Britain were straightforward and perfectly trustworthy. The British never understood that Russia, too, had her prestige to consider. The Russian government could not allow Russian lives and property to be endangered nor allow the flow of Russian trade to be disturbed. Having presented demands or ultimata to the Persian government she could not then withdraw without a serious loss of face. Public opinion had to be considered, even in Russia. Isvolski was sensitive to the slightest scepticism voiced about his policy in the Russian press and in court circles. Indeed his position was never secure. There were powerful factions in the government which opposed what they thought to be a conciliatory policy towards Britain. The Russian military staff were no more in favour of the 1907 Convention than was the High Command in India. They were firmly convinced that Russia had sacrificed more than she had gained by its terms. Britain was the traditional enemy whose ambitions beyond the frontiers of India could never be trusted. The military party at St Petersburg was strongly in favour of armed intervention in the north of Persia and after 1909 it rejected any suggestion of withdrawal. Isvolski survived a strong challenge in October 1908 only with the help of a glowing recommendation written by Edward VII to the Tsar. When he finally left office in 1910 his downfall was partially attributed to the fact that his policy had been too generous to British interests. His successor, Sazanoff, suffered the same insecurity. Sazanoff told the British Ambassador in January 1912 that he had done everything in his power to preserve the spirit of co-operation. Russian troops had not entered Tehran, Russia had refrained from giving military support to Mohammed Ali's attempt to regain his throne in 1911, and the Russian government had at last agreed to a joint advance of £200,000 to Persia. From the Russian viewpoint the occupation of the north of Persia was no more than was necessary for the preservation of law and order in an area adjacent to the Russian frontier.

More than anything else Russian statesmen feared the prospect of German intervention in the region. Germany had taken considerable interest in the Near East in the late nineteenth and early twentieth centuries. She had obtained a voice in the Ottoman Public Debt Administration, she had sent military missions to reform the Turkish army, and her financiers had lent money to, and received economic concessions from, the Turkish government. German trade with the Near East had expanded. Shipping services had been established. In the late 1890s the Persian Gulf had become a focus for German commercial activity. A vice-consulate was opened at Bushire in 1897.[1] And all this was just the beginning. After 1902 German influence in the Ottoman empire increased enormously due to the concession for the Bagdad railway.

Both Britain and Russia were apprehensive of this enterprise. The British feared that a railway down through Mesopotamia to an outlet on the Persian Gulf would bring both Germany and Turkey to challenge British supremacy in the region. The Russians were worried that the projected extension from Khanikin to Tehran would enable Germany to flood the markets of northern Persia with German goods and hence afford some pretext for interference in the Russian sphere. Neither Britain nor Russia wanted the Persians to grant railway concessions to the Germans. In April 1910 the two legations presented a note to the Persian government to the effect that Britain and Russia would permit no concession being given to the subjects of a third power which might prove injurious to their own political or strategic interests. Though the Germans claimed that their interest in Persia was strictly commercial this was plainly untrue. The German government refused to recognise the 1907 Convention and it always hoped to drive a wedge between Britain and Russia in Persian affairs which might disrupt the *entente* in Europe. The Russians were more alarmed by the prospect of German interference in Persia than were the British. The harsh conditions concerning railway concessions which the Russians demanded in return for any loan to the Persian government stemmed from their determination to acquire for themselves an option on all railway construction in the north of Persia and to keep out the Germans. Isvolski was under considerable pressure from the German Ambassador in 1910 to make some provision for the construction of the Khanikin-Tehran railway. Sazanoff reluctantly agreed to this by the terms of the Potsdam agreement in August 1911. In return he gained German recognition of the 1907 Convention and thereby of Russia's special interests in the north of Persia.

Russia's fear of the growing power of Germany, both in the Near East and in Europe in the late 1900s, explains a great deal as to her policy in Persia. By no means, though, does it account for all of it. Russian agents in the country often acted independently of St. Petersburg and of their Tehran legation. Russian officials were disturbed by the constitutional ideas which were spreading in Persia; they were by nature biased toward the old régime. Of course it was also difficult for Isvolski or Sazanoff to appreciate the problems with Parliament of

[1]   For the background to the expansion of German interests in the Near East see Henderson, 'German Economic Penetration', Martin, *German-Persian Diplomatic Relations;* and J. Marlowe, *The Persian Gulf in the Twentieth Century* (London, 1962), pp. 37-8.

which Grey so frequently complained. Sazanoff and the Tsar seemed taken aback in April 1914 when Grey refused to convert the 1907 Convention into a firm alliance between the two powers and gave as his reason the fact that neither public nor Parliamentary opinion in Britain would allow any binding commitment. The nature of Russian interests in Persia, the divisions within the Russian government, the fear of Germany, and the different perspective from which their officials assessed events in Persia must all be considered before any final judgement is passed on Russian actions. Grey was not alone in having to balance a variety of factors before deciding his policy in Persia.

Grey, like his predecessors at the Foreign Office, wanted no responsibilities in Persia. He made this clear in 1906. 'I will not go in for a forward policy in Persia', he wrote to Spring-Rice. 'We can only help those who help themselves. We might do a good deal to say hands off and help the independence of Persia, if it would show itself worthy of independence; but we can't let it lean upon us while it is rotten unless we are prepared to make a sort of protectorate, and this we are not'.[1] This was still his view in 1912. Admittedly it was proving very difficult to find a government in Persia capable of maintaining law and order: even so, Grey wrote, 'I do not regard a British occupation as inevitable, or as other than most undesirable'.[2] The Government of India welcomed this resolve to keep out of Persia's internal affairs. Lord Kitchener, the Commander in Chief of the Indian army, took the view that 'the less we have to do with such internal disturbances the better'. 'In my opinion', he continued, 'the maintenance of the *status quo* is preeminently the best policy which it would be the safest and most economical for us to adopt'.[3]

Few Foreign Secretaries can have faced quite such difficult problems as Grey did over Persia. Seen in retrospect, he was committed to two policies which were irreconcilable — the independence of Persia and the friendship of Russia. Moreover he was under considerable pressure from the radical wing of his party to do all that he could to aid the revolutionary cause in Persia. Personally, he was not averse to this; but there were definite reasons against interference. If he openly defended the constitutional movement then Russia would step in to save the Shah. Furthermore the tradition of foreign policy was against such intervention. Yet Persia again provides a study of how that tradition

1 Grey to Spring-Rice, 30 November 1906, *Spring-Rice Papers*, F.O. 800/241.
2 Grey to Scott, 21 September 1912, *Grey Papers*, F.O. 800/111.
3 Kitchener to Clarke, January 1906, *Kitchener Papers, Birdwood Collection*, 1906-14, mss. eur. D686/47.

could be modified to suit particular requirements. Not only that, it is a fine example of how the British government once more laid aside its principle of *laissez-faire* in economic matters by doing what it could to control the activities of private financiers in London in the matter of Persian loans. Just why the Foreign Office deviated from these guidelines emerges very clearly as the details of its policy are unravelled.

How far was Grey prepared to go in interfering in Persia's internal affairs? Understandably he wished to avoid any suspicion that he was doing so. That does not preclude the possibility, however, that Britain played some part in deciding the pattern of events in Persia in the late 1900s. In fact, it can be argued that British diplomacy in Persia between 1906 and 1909 was responsible for the eventual success of the revolutionary cause. Although circumstances arose in which the British by doing anything at all could have helped one side in the struggle or by doing absolutely nothing might have helped the other, the fact remains that in several ways British diplomacy, like British opinion in general tended to favour the Persian nationalists.[1]

This was so from the early days of the revolution. In 1906 the Tehran legation gave asylum to those who by their protest and their demonstration had incurred the wrath of the Shah and his régime. It was from the grounds of the British legation that the first successful movement for a constitution in Persia was launched. In the months which followed the occupation of the legation grounds by political refugees in July 1906, Spring-Rice pressed upon the Shah the need to forestall further political disturbances by granting a constitution. A constitution, he was sure, was the only way to save the Kajar dynasty. Whenever the opportunity presented itself the British Minister stressed the desirability of political reforms and the need for the Shah to honour such pledges as he had given in the past. The British government refused to be drawn by Russia into giving any guarantee for the survival of the Kajar family as the ruling house in Persia. After Mohammed Ali had been deposed in July 1909 the British were intent on getting him out of the country as soon as possible so that he would not become a focus for intrigue against the new régime. The British were partial to the Majlis and its leaders and eager to gain their esteem. 'Our policy should be to humour the Persian government', an Under-Secretary at the Foreign Office remarked in May 1910, 'and not to threaten and bully them'. Charles Hardinge fully agreed. 'The Persians are naturally disposed to be friendly to us as they do not suspect our intentions, and

---

[1] This point is explained very comprehensively in I. Klein, 'British Intervention in the Persian Revolution, 1905-09', *Historical Journal* 15 (1972) 731-52.

we must try by our friendly attitude to compensate for the dislike and distrust which the Persians feel for the Russians'.[1]

The fact that opinion in England was so strongly on the side of the revolutionaries had some bearing on official thinking. Every effort should be made to prevent Russia acting against the Majlis, Hardinge observed in 1908. If the Russians destroyed the chances for democracy in Persia then the future of the Liberal government in England, and of the 1907 Convention, would be precarious. The British dissuaded the Russians from giving military relief to the Shah when the nationalist armies were converging on Tehran in the summer of 1909. In a number of ways the British manipulated their policy of non-intervention to the advantage of the nationalist cause. Sympathy was converted into subtle support, and the Shah was denied the open assistance of the European powers which alone could have saved his absolute rule.

The best illustration of the British government's help for the Persian reform movement was in the field of finance. The Shah was denied access to British or to any sizable quantities of Russian capital; without foreign money his chances of putting down the revolution were almost non-existent. Grey's policy was clear. He was willing to co-operate with Russia in providing the Shah with money only on specified conditions — the most important of which was that any loan should be first approved by the Majlis. The British government advised the Russians against making separate advances to the Shah. To give him money unconditionally would have been to strengthen his opposition to the constitutional party and this, for the Foreign Office, was out of the question. The cabinet, in August 1908, approved in principle a joint Anglo-Russian loan of £400,000 to Persia on the strict condition 'that the money was not used to suppress the constitution but was advanced in such a way as to support it'.[2] Even when royalist forces seemed sure to capture the last nationalist stronghold of Tabriz in January 1909 Hardinge confirmed that no money would be lent to Persia until a constitutional régime was successfully installed. In May, with the nationalist armies approaching the capital, Mohammed Ali at last gave way to British diplomatic pressure. He restored the constitution and introduced financial reforms in return for the promise of an Anglo-Russian advance of £100,000.

In the years which followed the revolution British interference in Persian politics continued. Grey looked for strong and honest men in Persia who might be capable of holding together a fragmentary govern-

1 Minutes by Mallet and Hardinge on Marling to Grey, 4 May 1910, F.O. 371/954.

2 Minute by Grey on Marling to Grey, 1 August 1908, F.O. 371/501.

ment and of taking the necessary measures to bring about political stability, the rule of law, and sound financial administration. The search was unrewarding. The principal candidate was Saad-ed-Dowleh, whom the British forced the Shah to include in his government in May 1909. Three years later Britain and Russia agreed to push him as Prime Minister. Townley wrote from Tehran in November 1912 that, with his Russian colleague, he had 'worked hard to get people to swallow Saad-ed-Dowleh and agree to work with him'.[1] In the end, though, Grey had to back down. Saad-ed-Dowleh was hated in Persia and would never have been accepted as Prime Minister. He could only have been placed in office by armed force and this was quite beyond the bounds of practicality. 'Unofficial pressure' was the extent to which the Foreign Office was prepared to go — as indeed it did in April 1910 when Barclay tried to prevent the appointment of an extremist member to the Persian Cabinet.[2] The Foreign Office also looked to the prospect of European advisers in Persia as a means of exerting influence over financial administration.

If British policy is considered in the light of tradition a consistent pattern does emerge. The guide-line of non-intervention was made flexible with respect to the nationalist movement: conveniently enough, it was only invoked and strictly adhered to in respect of any support for the Shah. There was more than one reason why that was so. First, Britain had never been able to exercise much persuasion at Tehran; the Shah and the Persian court had long been under the influence of Russian diplomacy. Britain's position in Persia relied more on contacts between the legation and the clerical party and with the urban middle classes who regarded Russian policy with the greatest alarm. It also depended on Britain's ties with the tribes of the south — particularly the Sheikh of Mohammerah and the Bakhtiari khans. These chieftains resented royal authority. They were anti-dynastic, and, in the case of the Bakhtiaris, they were at the forefront of the revolutionary movement. To countenance the Shah would have been to sacrifice all influence among these powerful elements in Persia. The British were far more likely to act in concert with these groups than with the old régime.

Secondly, the British government could not remain indifferent to growing criticism at home. Had the Persian revolution failed, and had British diplomacy appeared to work hand in glove with Russia to shore up an autocratic Shah, Grey's position would have been difficult.

1   Townley to Nicolson, 27 November 1912, *Nicolson Papers,* F.O. 800/361.
2   Barclay to Grey, 17 April 1910, and minute by Norman on Nicolson to Grey, 3 May 1910, F.O. 371/954.

Nicolson told Townley, in July 1912, that 'we are always worried by thoughts of how our action will be viewed below the gangway of the House of Commons'.[1] The government's weakness was increased by the fact that it had no effective speaker with any knowledge of Persian affairs in the House of Lords. By the late 1900s the British also had to consider the tide of Moslem opinion in India. Certainly if Britain had joined with Russia in suppressing the nationalist movement in Persia the repercussions for the Government of India could have been very serious. Again it made no sense to do anything which might strengthen the Shah. The government was always under pressure to smooth the path for a constitutional régime in Persia and to counter Russian opposition to it whenever possible.

Thirdly, British officials realised that the time for change had come. The old régime was spent and the Shah reigned only as a Russian puppet whose sympathies were invariably unreliable. Charles Hardinge sensed this at the beginning of the revolution. 'It is useless to attempt to repair the Persian "administrative machine" which is worn out', he advised Grey in 1906. 'It is better to await developments with a view to providing a new one. We shall probably not have to wait long'.[2] On coming into office Grey had already decided that support for the *status quo* was useless and that all attempts to bolster up the régime in power, either diplomatically or financially, were doomed to fail. 'The present government in Persia is incapable and practically bankrupt: the money lent would not in the long run save the government or do any good to the country. The utmost it could do would be to stave off a crisis for a few weeks or months; at the end of which time another loan would be required with just as little prospect of doing any permanent good'. 'I see no object in making special efforts to defer this crisis', he continued. 'On the contrary, the sooner it comes the less chance will there be of Russia under present conditions taking advantage of it to interfere in the internal affairs of Persia'.[3] Grey was convinced that constitutional government would strengthen Persia: in fact he saw it as the only hope. His refusal to lend money until a constitutional régime had been installed was, as he saw it, in the best interest of Persia — and of Britain too. Charles Hardinge hoped that royalist troops would fail to overcome the nationalist defence of Tabriz in 1909 since any temporary success would harden the Shah's resistance to the reform movement. In the long term the Shah had no prospect of restoring order by the use of force. Barclay, in Tehran, was even more

1   Nicolson to Townley, 1 July 1912, *Nicolson Papers,* F.O. 800/357.
2   Minute by Hardinge on Grant-Duff to Grey, 28 February 1906, F.O. 371/107.
3   Memorandum by Grey, 18 December 1905, *Grey Papers,* F.O. 800/92.

extreme. He agreed with the Foreign Office that 'constitutional checks on the present despicable Shah' was perhaps the best that could be hoped for; but he would settle for that only because, at the time, he saw no leader in the country who was capable of turning Mohammed Ali out of Persia once and for all.[1]

Just as a despotic Shah would always be the instrument of Russian policy, so a constitutional régime would allow the growth of British influence. 'We have a powerful ally in the National Assembly', an official at the Foreign Office optimistically remarked in 1907.[2] The British government was still committed to a policy of halting the spread of Russian influence through Persia and of maintaining the country as a neutral buffer state. Admittedly Grey now relied on the 1907 Convention to try to limit Russian power to the northern sphere, but he still looked to Persia to continue functioning as an independent nation, free from the troubles and disorders which might provide the Russians with an excuse for military occupation. When British diplomacy worked in favour of the Persian nationalists it was not an empty sympathy which was expressed. The British government had to consider its standing at home, its influence with the various groups within Persian society, and the effects of its policy on the feelings of its subjects in India. It also weighed the principle of non-intervention against its political aims in Persia over the past century. The 'buffer state' required an administration at Tehran which was capable of keeping law and order.

To assess the extent to which Grey's policy represented a departure from accepted standards of official conduct it is necessary also to examine the precise way in which he used his influence to control the supply of foreign capital to the Persian government. Grey developed a clear policy with regard to Persian loans. By the arrangement of 1906 Britain and Russia agreed to advance £400,000 to the Persian government. The British share would mean payment from Treasury funds in London, following the precedents which had been set by the Anglo-Indian loans of 1903 and 1904. Isvolski was eager to make the loan in order to forestall any moves by German financiers. Grey, on the other hand, was at first less enthusiastic about lending to Persia. 'I do not like lending money to a country which is going downhill and getting deeper and deeper into debt', he wrote to Nicolson at St. Petersburg, 'It means that some day we shall have to realise our securities by force and undertake new responsibilities'.[3] But Grey's reluctance was overcome in the light of other considerations: here was a splendid oppor-

1 Barclay to Hardinge, 28 April 1909, *Hardinge Papers*, vol. 15.

2 Minute by Norman on Spring-Rice to Grey, 23 April 1907, F.O. 371/305.

3 Grey to Nicolson, 3 October 1906, *Grey Papers*, F.O. 800/72.

tunity to co-operate with Russia and hence to prepare the way for a wider understanding. Furthermore, the Shah had just granted a Persian constitution and Grey considered him more worthy of support than he had been back in December 1905. However the loan never came off. The Shah dared not accept the offer for fear of public disturbances in Persia and the outright opposition of the Majlis. All the same, the offer of a joint advance remained open to the Persian government until the Shah's *coup d'état* in June 1908. Thereafter the Shah's need of funds was the lever by which the British government forced him to restore the constitution.

Fortunately for Grey the Shah could not go elsewhere to borrow money. The Russians supplied him with some small advances in 1907 but, by and large, the Russian government at that time was in no position to provide the sums which the Shah desperately required. The only other possibility was German capital, but help from this quarter was unlikely. Certainly both the British and Russian governments were worried by rumours that German financiers were to help establish a Persian national bank. It was doubtful, though, that the Germans had the resources to spare. Persia was really a sideline of German activity in the Near East compared to the growth of her influence in the Ottoman empire. German aspirations in Persia were limited to sowing discord between Britain and Russia, and the Bagdad railway project proved to be more than a sufficient opening for German foreign investment.

The only other source to which the Shah could turn were private banks in London. Here lay Grey's difficulty. Obviously Grey could refuse to lend money to Persia from the British treasury, but how could he stop British bankers, should they wish to do so, from lending to the Shah during the revolution or, after July 1909, from lending to the new régime on terms which he disapproved? This was all-important. Whatever money the Shah received strengthened his opposition to the nationalist cause and thereby frustrated British attempts to establish a constitutional government at Tehran. Whether Persia continued to disintegrate under a despotic Shah (and was eventually to be formally partitioned between Britain and Russia) or whether a new régime could come to power depended on the ability of the British government to control a number of private financiers in London who had suddenly appeared upon the scene and who were all zealous to lend. After 1909 the survival and stability of the nationalist government depended in its turn, in Grey's judgement, upon the way in which it raised its foreign loans.

To veto the supply of money to Persia would mean a degree of involvement in the affairs of the City far beyond the bounds of normal practice. The London money market had enjoyed freedom from political supervision throughout the nineteenth century. British governments had had no wish and no real ability to control the flow of capital abroad: as late as 1914 Grey, in public, was quite emphatic that the principle of *laissez-faire* still held good. But to ignore the activities of private financiers was easier said than done. After 1909 Grey could no longer afford to keep out of the affairs of the City. This did not apply only to Persia. In 1910, for instance, the Foreign Office stopped Sir Ernest Cassel's National Bank of Turkey from lending money to the Turkish government. In the case of China, after 1911, Grey was obliged to restrain a number of financiers from lending to the new republic and to give an unprecedented measure of preferential treatment to the Hongkong and Shanghai Bank. These steps made nonsense of the government's official declarations. The truth was, as Grey confessed, that frequently the supply of funds abroad could not be considered apart from the political implications. 'Sick men' such as China and Turkey were exactly the areas where political and financial affairs were inseparable and where it had become impossible to abide by the old principles of diplomatic practice. Persia was a further and perhaps the clearest illustration of the changes which were taking place in the approach of British officials to high finance. A strict control of the London money market had become essential if Grey's political aims were to be achieved.

Until the revolution ended in July 1909 the only British bank interested in Persia's finances was the Imperial Bank of Persia. But even this bank presented the Foreign Office with problems in respect of Persian loans. The Bank was initially unimpressed by Grey's resolution that the British government would not lend money to Persia until a constitutional régime was in power. Nor were the Bank's business operations always in accordance with Grey's wish to encourage the reform movement. When the Bank proposed to collect outstanding debts from some prominent nationalists at Tehran in March 1907 the Foreign Office strongly advised the Bank to drop its claims for the moment. 'The Imperial Bank of Persia would have done well to consult us before taking so serious a step', one of the clerks remarked.[1] The Bank was informed that, though Grey had no desire to interfere in its business affairs, the action which was now proposed would not be welcomed by the Majlis or by the popular movement at large and it would reflect badly on Britain.

The Bank relented and took this matter no further. However it

1 Minute by Norman on Spring-Rice to Grey, 21 March 1907, F.O. 371/305.

found itself at loggerheads with the Foreign Office again in February 1909. On this occasion the British and Russian banks in Persia had come to an arrangement which would have provided £70,000 for the Shah in his struggle against the revolutionaries in return for an agreement about the repayment of his debts. Barclay condemned the transaction in the strongest terms. 'It would not have failed to prolong the agony of this detestable government, stiffening and strengthening the Shah and discouraging the nationalists', he wrote from Tehran.[1] In London, the Foreign Office put a damper on the venture straight away; it even managed to persuade the Russian government to restrain the Russian bank. Charles Hardinge replied to Barclay that the Imperial Bank had now agreed to reject the proposals which the Shah had made and that nothing more would be heard of the scheme. 'It was altogether a most uncomfortable position for us', Hardinge reflected. 'The Bank of Persia evidently wished to do a little speculation in the hope of eventually recovering their larger debt'. The Foreign Office had had no means of intervening officially but Hardinge had explained the views of the Foreign Office to the Bank. The manager, Hardinge continued, 'who is a very patriotic fellow, has jumped to it today, and has washed his hands of it. It would have been very unfortunate if we had thus provided the Shah with the sinews of war'.[2] In declining the business the Bank had acted contrary to the interests of its shareholders. The government should remember, the Tehran manager wrote to his superior in London, 'we scrupulously carried out their wishes to our own detriment and did all in our power to further their policy in Persia'.[3]

The Foreign Office did not end its interference in the financing of Persia with the overthrow of Mohammed Ali. In the years which followed, the supply of money to the new regime grew in importance. The joint advance of £400,000 was still on offer though the Majlis had reservations about borrowing from the British and Russian governments. Now that Mohammed Ali had been deposed and a new constitutional government was at last in power the Foreign Office was keen to lend. Persia needed foreign capital and Grey became more and more impatient with the Majlis and its unbending attitude. 'They cannot keep their pride and get money', he remarked in February 1910. 'They must forego one or the other'.[4]

When Grey offered money to the new Persian government he did so

1 Barclay to Hardinge, 15 February 1909, *Hardinge Papers*, F.O. 800/192.

2 Hardinge to Barclay, 16 February 1909, *Hardinge Papers*, vol. 17.

3 Wood to Newell, 14 August 1909, enclosed in Jackson to Mallet, 8 September 1909, F.O. 371/719.

4 Minute by Grey on Barclay to Grey, 28 February 1910, F.O. 371/947.

for very specific reasons. First, the provision of funds by Britain and Russia (on the fairly generous terms which he suggested) was meant to win the confidence of the Majlis and prevent the Persians from trying to borrow German capital. Secondly, the money was to be used for the establishment of an efficient Persian gendarmerie to restore order in the south of Persia. Thirdly, the joint advance would play a part in the economic and administrative rejuvenation of Persia. The money would tide over the Persian government until the revenues and taxes from the provinces and the customs receipts were collected again, and until such a time, therefore, as Persia could offer adequate securities to enable a private and much larger loan to be raised in the London money market. The terms of any loan were crucial. If money were given unconditionally it would almost certainly be squandered or else it would find its way into the pockets of Persian officials. Grey wanted strict controls on the expenditure of money lent to Persia in order to ensure that it was used to bring about political stability in the country.

Grey had already stopped the Imperial Bank of Persia from lending money in 1909. In 1910 he faced further difficulties with British financiers since a number of City houses now wished to enter the field of Persian loans. Why this sudden interest in Persia on the part of private capital? Certainly it was in marked contrast to the horror with which private financiers had viewed the possibility of investment in Persia in previous years. Any new government in the nineteenth or early twentieth centuries, though, and particularly those based upon liberal or constitutional principles, enjoyed a honeymoon period with the London money market. The new republics of Latin America in the early decades of the nineteenth century were cases in point. Equally, the revolution in China at the end of 1911 was to whet the appetites of a number of banking houses which had expressed no interest whatever in the old régime. A few constitutional concessions by the Tsar after the 1905 revolution, combined of course with the 1907 agreement with Britain, opened the London money market to the Russian government in a way that had been inconceivable before.

Before 1910 no investor had relished the prospect of lending money to a Russian puppet Shah: a constitutional régime, however, was a different matter — particularly when its leaders, and indeed the nation as a whole, looked to Britain in admiration, in gratitude, and for guidance. There was also a chance of improvement in the economic and political condition of the country. Moreover, to earn the goodwill of the Majlis in its early and most trying years might reap substantial rewards for enterprising banking houses in the way of transactions later on. The British government was known to approve the cause of constitutional reform in Persia. It had declared its support for the country's integrity and two years earlier it had signed an agreement with Russia binding the Russian government to the same purpose. Surely in these circumstances a Persian recovery would be possible? Things looked a lot brighter for Persia towards the end of 1909 and in 1910 and British capitalists were not slow to appreciate the changes which were taking place. It was to take a few months, even a year or two, before those illusions were totally shattered.

To Grey's way of thinking these City houses had one thing in common: they all put in jeopardy his grand design for the rejuvenation of Persia under official British and Russian auspices. Messrs. Samuel were one such firm. They were a respectable merchant banking house bent on extending their operations in Asia. In 1909 they had tried unsuccessfully to enter the field of Chinese railway finance when a number of British houses were tendering for the right to build the important trunk line from Hankow, in the Yangtsze Valley, down to Canton. In March 1910 a representative of the firm called at the Foreign Office to discuss their proposal to join in a loan of up to £500,000 to the Persian government. 'We have no wish to encourage them', Charles Hardinge decided at once, 'as to do so would be prejudicial to the success of the joint advance'.[1] Samuel were told that the British government would agree to no loan to Persia which competed for the same security as that which was available for the Anglo-Russian advance and that proved sufficient to dissuade them from going any further.

A second banking house to express interest in a loan was Messrs. Crisp & Company. Crisp were essentially stock brokers whose main interest lay in Russia — particularly financing Russian railways in the 1900s. The Foreign Office promptly informed them that so long as a joint advance was under consideration, and as long as the Persian government was in arrears in debt repayments to the British and Russian governments and to the British and Russian banks in Persia, it would allow no hypothecation of Persian revenues for any private advance. Messrs Boulton, a reasonably prosperous banking and trading firm operating largely in Venezuela, was told precisely the same thing when it enquired about the attitude of the British government to Persian loans. These conditions, an official observed, 'will practically exclude other would-be lenders'.[2] Yet others did appear. The International Oriental Syndicate approached the Foreign Office in April 1910 with

1 Minute by Hardinge on Barclay to Grey, 7 March 1910, F.O. 371/947.
2 Minute by Maxwell on Messrs. Crisp & Co. to Foreign Office, 4 April 1910, F.O. 371/957.

like proposals. This was not a powerful firm however. The Syndicate was generally regarded as nothing more than a speculative venture and was represented in Tehran by a shady character called Osborne. The Foreign Office realized that 'we can always put sufficient pressure on Persia to prevent them from having any dealings with them'.[1] So far, the Foreign Office had not been too much troubled by City financiers. All had given way when discouraged by the officials whom they had seen. After April, however, the Foreign Office had to deal with the far more reputable firm of Seligman Brothers.

Seligman was a small but well-known house which specialised in credit business. The name had first appeared in London in the 1860s as an offshoot of the great New York banking firm, J. & W. Seligman & Company. In 1897 the London firm was established as an independent business and its rise to some prominence was due in part to its carefully nurtured ties with the house of Rothschild. Seligman had one advantage with respect to Persian finance. The firm was well regarded by the Majlis since it had been sufficiently astute to engage as its agent in Tehran an Englishman, W.A. Moore, who had been one of the nationalist heroes at the siege of Tabriz in the early months of 1909. The problem which Seligman now posed for the Foreign Office was not entirely unforeseen. 'Supposing a strong syndicate came forward', an Under-Secretary mused in April 1910, 'it will be very difficult, if not impossible for us to discourage them'.[2] Seligman was such a syndicate and it could tempt the Persian government with an offer of up to £2,500,000. This was a much sterner test for Grey. The question was whether he could still defend his political objectives and just how far he would go to try to prevent Seligman from entering the field.

Grey told Seligman that no revenues over which the British or Russian governments held a lien could be given as security. The same applied to liens held by the Imperial Bank of Persia and the Russian Banque des Prêts. On 31 May 1910 Seligman was informed that the British government would sanction no private loan to Persia while negotiations for a joint advance by the British and Russian governments were underway. Seligman's agent at Tehran went ahead however. The legation tried to stop his initiative to sign a contract with the Persian government by telling him abruptly that 'an offer of à loan would be harmful to our policy'. 'I explained it would be harmful', the Chargé d'affaires wrote to the Foreign Office, 'because I thought it possible that the Persians would, *malgré tout*, apply to the two powers and would therefore give them an opportunity of showing that

1 Foreign Office minute on Wolff to Hardinge, 8 April 1910, F.O. 371/954.
2 Minute by Mallet on Hardinge to Grey, 20 April 1910, F.O. 371/954.

their professions of friendship were genuine and sincere, and so winning the confidence of the Persians'.[1] In July, however, the negotiations for a joint advance broke down. Suddenly the Foreign Office sensed the danger of the Germans stepping in to provide a loan and so Seligman was told that the British government would not now oppose its trans-action after all.

But Seligman was intricately involved with foreign banking houses, and this transaction, as the Foreign Office soon discovered, would come about from money which it planned to raise in Holland, France, Switzerland, and Germany. It was even suspected that Seligman was working with the powerful Deutsche Bank. Seligman's loan took on a menacing appearance once again. 'I do not think we can agree in prin-ciple to this', the Foreign Office decided. 'The capital will not be British, and Germans will be interested'. Grey was worried about the security which would be arranged. 'Would it not give the other powers a footing in the Gulf?' he wrote to Barclay in Tehran. Barclay replied that indeed it would. 'All this points to discouraging messrs. Selig-man', one of the clerks at the Foreign Office decided in September 1910.[2] Before the scheme could be allowed to go ahead the Foreign Office would need to know the extent of foreign co-operation, the proportion of the bonds which would be held abroad, and the composi-tion of the board of directors of the firm.

Even after Seligman had given satisfactory answers the Foreign Office continued to view the project with disfavour. Grey told a lead-ing Persian politician who was in London at the time that he thought 'the Persian government were going on a wrong track in imagining that they could get set upon their feet by appealing to Seligman'. 'I said that they had much better apply for a loan, not guaranteed, but under British and Russian auspices', Grey wrote to Barclay.[3] In October the Persian government proposed to borrow £1,200,000 from Seligman, secured by a first lien on the southern customs. This would unquestion-ably have given the firm a prior claim to those revenues over both the British government and the Imperial Bank of Persia. The Foreign Office decided that 'it is not at all desirable that the Seligman loan should succeed'. The question was: 'what is the best way of choking Seligman off?' 'We know very well that there is a risk of the Germans coming into the Seligman loan if it comes off', an official remarked,

1   Marling to Mallet, 1 July 1910, F.O. 371/958.

2   Minute by Maxwell on Seligman Brothers to Foreign Office, 15 September 1910; Grey to Barclay, 15 September 1910; minute by Norman on Barclay to Grey, 16 September 1910; F.O. 371/958.

3   Grey to Barclay, 12 October 1910, *Grey Papers,* F.O. 800/70.

'and we hope to prevent it'. After 20 October 1910 that task was made much easier. The Imperial Bank of Persia began negotiations for a similar loan and Grey told Seligman that the British government would support no other financial house while those negotiations were in progress. Seligman dropped the business at the end of the month. The Foreign Office told Seligman quite plainly that any continuation of its transaction would be regarded by the British government 'as prejudicial to British interests'. Grey had used the Imperial Bank of Persia to block the way for Seligman's loan. Seligman had 'behaved quite decently',[1] as the Foreign Office conceded, but its loan had posed a threat to Grey's policy in several important respects.

In the first place it would have obstructed a joint advance from the British and Russian governments. What is more there were no controls attached to Seligman's offer. There was no way to ensure that the money would be used to institute an efficient administration and the rule of order throughout Persia. Finally, Seligman's loan would have interfered with the liens of the British government and the Imperial Bank of Persia on the southern customs revenues. Because the loan did not fit Grey's conception of how to strengthen Persia he had no hesitation in trying to stop it. When it realized that the Persian government would not accept a joint advance from Britain and Russia the Foreign Office turned to its trusted agent in Persia, the Imperial Bank, to provide private British capital. The contract which the Bank began to negotiate in October 1910 was finally accepted by the Majlis in May 1911. In actively discouraging loans to Persia by a number of British banking houses, and in giving preferential support to the Imperial Bank of Persia, the Foreign Office had discarded the principle that it should not interfere in the world of private finance. Grey met with difficulty in using his influence, but he had no option. If he wished to continue to use the supply of foreign capital to restore stability in Persia then that supply had to be strictly controlled. Ultimately his efforts to maintain the independence of the country depended upon it.

Critics of the government, however, were not convinced that Grey's policy aimed to bring the constitutionalist party to power. That was scarcely suprising, for they could not know of his subtle efforts to break the Shah's opposition to the revolution nor of his manoeuvrings with City houses which were intended to give the nationalist government a chance of survival. They complained bitterly about the plight of

[1] Minute by Mallet on Barclay to Nicolson, 18 October 1910; minute by Maxwell on Barclay to Grey, 19 October 1910; Seligman Brothers to Foreign Office, 28 October 1910; minute by Lindsay on Seligman Brothers to Foreign Office, 7 November 1910; F.O. 371/958.

Persia and about the duplicity of Russian officials. In the eyes of liberal England Grey was sacrificing Persia for the sake of the Anglo-Russian *entente*. He seemed to do nothing to protect the independence of the country or the newly-won freedom of the Persian people when Russian forces occupied Tabriz and presented outrageous ultimata to the government at Tehran. But were these reproaches justified? Was it true, as the Indian authorities, the liberal press, and radical opinion in Parliament all claimed, that Grey's only concern was to maintain at any price the friendship of a nation whose statesmen cared for nothing but conquest and control in Central Asia?

It was easy to condemn Grey for not defending Persia's liberties. It was more difficult to appreciate the problems which he encountered in that country. There can be no doubt that the Foreign Office viewed Russian activity in Persia in the late 1900s with considerable misgivings. From the early days of the Convention even its architects had found the Russian government an exasperating partner. 'It is extraordinary how difficult it is to get the Russians to work honestly and loyally anywhere', Charles Hardinge wrote in June 1908, 'one always has to be continually at them'.[1] The behaviour of Russian agents in Persia was a perpetual threat to the success of the Anglo-Russian agreement but Grey was loth to complain to the Russian government. He did not wish to imply that Isvolski and Sazanoff were not acting in good faith: besides, he realised that such representations were useless. This put him in an awkward position at home. 'Grey has constantly, during the past year, had to appear in the House of Commons as the advocate of the Russian government', Hardinge wrote to Nicolson in October 1908. 'We have had to suppress the truth and resort to subterfuge at times to meet hostile public opinion', he continued. 'This is entirely owing to their lack of control over their officials'.[2] The presence of Russian troops in northern Persia was a serious embarrassment for the British government. So too were the dilatory proceedings of the Russian government when it came to the proposal to advance money to the Persian government after July 1909. British officials could never understand Russian policy. To their way of thinking Russia failed to see the importance of conciliating the Persian government and was totally oblivious to the hatred which Russian troops and agents engendered wherever they went. However Grey was not in a strong position to influence the actions of the Russian government. Since he wished to preserve the *entente* 'at all hazards' he had no sanction to apply.[3] When

1 Hardinge to Goschen, 30 June 1908, *Hardinge Papers*, vol. 13.
2 Hardinge to Nicolson, 20 October 1908, *Hardinge Papers*, vol. 13.
3 Nicolson to Goschen, 27 November 1911, *Nicolson Papers*, F.O. 800/352.

the Russian government was finally warned in October 1911 that the occupation of the northern provinces would endanger the whole understanding between the two powers it must have been fairly obvious that Grey was not in earnest. The British government had tied the fortunes of its foreign policy, and to some extent its success in Parliament, to a most uncertain ally.

Indeed, it seemed, Grey declined to represent the best interests of Persia to the Russian government. This was particularly so by the end of 1911 when it became apparent that the constitutional experiment in Tehran was doomed. He feared causing offence at St Petersburg and he feared the implications of a collapse of the Anglo-Russian *entente*. His detractors in the press and in Parliament could not understand that, Nicolson complained. 'They do not see that our understanding is of far more importance to us than it is to Russia, and were it to break down we should be confronted with innumerable difficulties, not only in Central Asia and Persia, but also in Europe'.[1] General hints were dropped and the wish of the British government to maintain a spirit of active co-operation was repeatedly stressed; but, for the most part, that was all that happened. Grey, Nicolson, and Charles Hardinge always thought primarily in terms of the politics of Europe. Russia was a counterpoise to the growing power of Germany and her friendship was essential. There were powerful factions at the Russian court whose sympathy lay with Germany and not with Britain. Complaints about Russian policy in Persia would provide a golden opportunity for German statesmen to revive the old spirit of Russo-German friendship.

Persia, and particularly the northern provinces, was by necessity a secondary consideration. Had British paramountcy in the Persian Gulf been seriously challenged things might have been different. But the Foreign Office was not prepared to sacrifice the 1907 Convention just for the northern part of Persia which it had already recognised as constituting a Russian zone of influence. Nicolson informed Barclay, in October 1911, that 'it would be disastrous to our foreign policy were the understandings between Russia, France, and ourselves to be weakened in any way whatsoever'.[2] Barclay saw the passage of events only from the narrow standpoint of Persia — as did the government's critics at home. Only weeks before the outbreak of war in 1914 Nicolson was still arguing along the same lines. Nothing was to be allowed to impair the Anglo-Russian understanding; the difficulties in Persia therefore had to be subordinated to its needs. Not everyone at the Foreign office agreed. One of the clerks in 1910 had failed to 'see the good of

---

1   Nicolson to Lowther, 15 January 1912, *Nicolson Papers,* F.O. 800/353.
2   Nicolson to Barclay, 24 October 1911, *Nicolson Papers,* F.O. 800/351.

having an *entente* with Russia if we are never to be allowed to express our views even in the mildest language'.[1] Charles Hardinge and Grey, however, had been quick to point out the folly of his ways. Such rumblings of enquiry were not voiced again until just before the war.

It can be argued that the British government sacrificed the interests of Persia for the sake of good Anglo-Russian relations on a number of occasions. Substantial evidence for this is to be found in Grey's response to the Russian occupation of the northern provinces. Isvolski, indeed, expressed his gratitude in November 1909 that 'H.M.G. are ready to do their best to make the Persian government amenable and conciliatory' over the matter.[2] When Russian troops were outside Tehran at the end of 1911, and Russia presented her ultimatum to the Persian government, the British legation advised that resistance to Russian pressure was useless and that Persia would be best served by Succumbing to Russia's demands.[3] When Russian forces bombarded the Meshed shrine in 1912 Grey's protests at St Petersburg could scarcely have been weaker. The same was true about reports of Russian atrocities in Tabriz in December 1911.

The dismissal of Morgan Shuster was perhaps the most obvious example of the British advising the Persian government to give way to Russian demands. The British government agreed in November 1911 that Shuster would have to be discarded and that Britain would not fight Russia's insistence upon it. If the Persians did not dismiss Shuster and Russian troops occupied Tehran the outcry in England would be so strong that the *entente* would undoubtedly be ruptured. Shuster was not the man for the job of financial adviser to the Persian government. The Foreign Office realised that 'trouble between ourselves and the Russians will continually be sowed until he goes'.[4] Though Grey had welcomed Shuster's appointment as a fine opportunity for the introduction of proper financial administration in Persia, Shuster had subsequently lost Grey's good-will by antagonising the Russians and so precipitating the advance of Russian troops towards Tehran which placed such a considerable strain upon Anglo-Russian friendship.

Linked with Shuster's downfall was the suppression of the Majlis in December 1911. The British government agreed to this as well. The Majlis had proved to be a source of friction between the Persian and Russian governments; it was an institution which the Russians had

1   Minute by Norman on Nicolson to Grey, 13 February 1910, F.O. 371/952.
2   Nicolson to Hardinge, 3 November 1909, *Hardinge Papers*, vol. 16.
3   Kazemzadeh, p. 577.
4   Foreign Office minute on Barclay to Grey, 8 November 1911, F.O. 371/1199.

always wished to see abolished. There were those in official circles in London who questioned this conciliatory policy. The King's private secretary was among them. It was not just a question of hostile public opinion at home but one of morality with respect to Persia. 'I only hope we won't be dragged into any further interferences with Persia's internal affairs in order to placate Russia', he wrote to Nicolson at the end of December 1911. 'We cannot oppose all reform and progress in the country in order to maintain the Convention'.[1] In 1907 the Viceroy of India had been of much the same opinion. 'We have acted hand in glove with the most abominable autocracy of modern times', he wrote after the Convention had been signed. 'In Persia, we have shown, to say the least of it, little sympathy with the ambitions or the patriotism of its people and have rather appeared to stand by and shut our eyes to the intrigues of the great power to the north'.[2] The Foreign Office seemed to have ignored Russian activities in the north and Russian intrigues to save Mohammed Ali Shah. Even the indignity of having the British legation surrounded by Cossacks in June 1908 had not prompted Grey to place any great strain upon the understanding with Russia.

Yet Grey's policy in Persia must not be reviled as being simply one of accommodating Russian aspirations for the sake of the 1907 Convention and the balance of power in Europe. The understanding with Russia was also part and parcel of his Persian policy and that policy was in itself important. Persia's role had not significantly changed. The Foreign Office reassured the India Office in 1912 that it still worked to keep Russian influence away from those areas of Persia which were essential for the defence of India. Grey still saw Persia as a buffer state between Russia and the Indian frontier. When he acquiesced in arbitrary Russian action in the north of Persia to preserve Anglo-Russian friendship he did so only because he saw that friendship as being ultimately a better safeguard for the British empire. What is more, Britain could not maintain the integrity of Persia by force. 'Our only chance of maintaining the independence of Persia is to be on the friendliest possible terms with Russia', the Ambassador at St Petersburg wrote to Nicolson in 1912. 'We shall then be able to exercise a restraining influence on her and to keep her in line with us'.[3]

This was what Grey had tried to do. Spring-Rice had to concede in November 1907 that had it not been for her negotiations with Britain in the past year Russia would have intervened far more forcefully in

1   Stamfordham to Nicolson, 27 December 1911, *Nicolson Papers,* F.O. 800/ 353.

2   Minto to Morley, 9 October 1907, *Morley Papers,* D573/13.

3   Buchanan to Nicolson, 24 January 1912, *Nicolson Papers,* F.O. 800/353.

the Persian revolution.[1] Grey tried to discourage Russian troops from entering northern Persia; after 1909 he always urged that they be withdrawn. Grey's pressure on the Russian government after October 1908 delayed Russian forces crossing the Persian frontier for fully six months. In November 1911 the embassy in Russia considered that 'it is certain that nothing but British influence prevents a Russian occupation'.[2] Had it not been for Grey's representations, the acting Russian Foreign Minister remarked, Russian troops would long since have been in Tehran. Grey wanted Russian co-operation to establish a strong central government at Tehran. He therefore declined all suggestion of saving Mohammed Ali Shah and he tried to convince the Russian government that it should make the task of the new régime as light as possible. He induced the Russian government to join him in insisting that money should be lent to Persia, before 1909, only on condition that it would not be used to suppress the constitution and that its expenditure would be properly controlled. After 1909 he tried to dissuade the Russians from attaching conditions about economic concessions to any joint advance by the two governments. Charles Hardinge was certainly content with the way in which the Foreign Office had handled the crisis in Persia in July 1909. The Russian government had not interfered militarily to keep Mohammed Ali on his throne, 'but we are confident that, had it not been for the check that we imposed on Isvolski, he would have gone a great deal further than would have suited us'. [3]

In short, the British government realised that it could not work against Russia in Persia; its best policy therefore was to try to work with her. The 'buffer state' could not be maintained by force of arms, but only by convincing the Russian government that the independence of Persia and the restoration of political stability and economic prosperity there was as much to Russia's interest as to that of everyone else. That, in essence, was Grey's policy. It can be condemned as being idealistic or as an attempt to balance far too many incompatible considerations. For the Foreign Office, however, it was a case of *faute de mieux*. The British could do very little in Persia and what they could do was confined to the area adjacent to the Persian Gulf. By 1914 the 'buffer state' was quite beyond their means. It was a bonus, in fact, that there was still a central government in Tehran at all. Grey could congratulate himself that Persia remained nominally independent. Without the Russian Convention it is quite possible that that would not have been so.

1   Spring-Rice to Browne, November 1907, *Browne Papers,* file: letters from Persia 1905-09.
2   O'Beirne to Nicolson, 2 November 1911, *Nicolson Papers,* F.O. 800/351.
3   Hardinge to O'Beirne, 21 July 1909, *Hardinge Papers,* vol. 17.

6

THE SOUTH OF PERSIA 1906 – 1914

By 1912 Persia had almost disintegrated. After the departure of Morgan Shuster at the end of 1911 the central government existed in little more than name. With Russian troops occupying the northern provinces the independence of the country was really a pretence. The government was bankrupt, its troops and servants were unpaid, and it was unable to quell the disorders which seemed to become more widespread all the time. Many British officials now believed that European control of Persia's finances was indispensable for restoring stability; the problem here was that the Persians refused to agree to such an indignity and the Russians showed no enthusiasm for constructive co-operation. The 'buffer state' remained British policy, even though since 1907 that policy had depended on working with Russia rather than opposing her. Grey, however, was under no illusion as to Persia's chances of survival. The 'buffer state' became increasingly merely a first line of defence and less and less the means upon which the British relied to defend their interests in the Persian Gulf. Under Lansdowne, of course, the Foreign Office had already done a great deal to try to create the basis for a second buffer zone in the territory inland from the Gulf littoral. After 1906 those efforts were multiplied. The British government turned its attention to the south of Persia to prepare for the eventuality that Russian influence could no longer be confined to the northern sphere.

In the early 1900s Lansdowne had used economic measures to strengthen Britain's position in the south of Persia. He had taken steps to facilitate the growth of British trade in the southern and central provinces, he had supported the Imperial Bank, and he had tightened Britain's grip upon the use of the customs revenues of the Gulf ports as security for loans. Grey followed in his footsteps. As far as the southern customs were concerned he went to considerable trouble to ensure that British liens were not infringed, by discouraging and effectively preventing a number of financial houses from lending money to the Persian government. In 1908, when the Persian government proposed to give a subsidy to the German school at Tehran, the Foreign Office objected because that subsidy was to be guaranteed by the revenues of the southern customs. 'In any future question involving security on the customs', an official remarked, 'the Germans will have a claim to be consulted'. Hitherto, he continued, 'we have jealously guarded the customs revenue as security for our loans and resisted for years any

Russian lien on them'. Grey replied that 'we must assert our prior lien if need be'.[1]

It was also important that the liens held by the British government and by the Imperial Bank should not be permitted to expire because of the early repayment of loans. If this occurred then those revenues would be free to be pledged as security for other transactions and the struggle to keep them under British control would need to be fought all over again. It was a source of considerable satisfaction to the Foreign Office that the terms of British loans to Persia were such that repayment could be delayed until 1925. When the Persian government asked for more time in which to begin loan repayments in April 1910 officials there were more than ready to oblige. 'In fact it is of advantage that the debt should not be repaid', an Under-Secretary observed.[2] In that case the lien on the southern customs could be retained indefinitely – a point on which, Charles Hardinge decided, 'we shall accept no compromise'.[3] In October 1910 the date for repayment of the British government's loans of 1903 and 1904 was extended beyond 1928. When the Imperial Bank of Persia began its loan negotiations with the Persian government in the same month there was the prospect of an even firmer hold over the Gulf customs. The India Office was particularly keen that the Bank's loan should be secured on the remaining surplus of the southern customs revenues and that the new lien should run for fifty years. 'The object of the condition is to enable us to retain our lien on the customs, and so keep out Germans and others for the longest possible time', an official there remarked. 'It is a political object'.[4]

Like Lansdowne in the early 1900s Grey was also concerned for the prosperity of British trade in the southern and central provinces of Persia. It was vital to keep open the roads which carried that trade – principally those between Bushire and Ispahan, the Bakhtiari road from Ahwaz to Ispahan, and the road north of Ispahan towards the capital. In addition there was the trade route which ran northwards from the Karun River through Luristan. By 1910 the south of Persia was in a state of anarchy. The roads were controlled by gangs of bandits and the local governor at Ispahan could do nothing to remedy that state of affairs. A large caravan carrying British and Indian merchandise was

1   Minutes by Mallet and Grey on Marling to Grey, 13 March 1908, F.O. 371/502.
2   Minute by Mallet on Marling to Grey, 25 April 1910, F.O. 371/956.
3   Hardinge to Nicolson, 26 April 1910, *Nicolson Papers,* F.O. 800/343.
4   Hirtzel to Ritchie, 12 November 1910, I.O. L/P&S/10/11, 1903, file: 4238.

captured on the road from Yezd to Meshed early in that year. The road between Ispahan and Tehran was also judged to be unsafe. That from the coast at Bushire up to Ispahan was no longer passable without armed escort. As a further symptom of disorder and a further blow to British commerce, the Indo-European Telegraph Department's line in Seistan was destroyed and the British staff put to flight. Mail robberies were frequent; tribal strife was rampant as old scores could easily be settled in the conditions which prevailed. In August 1911 an official at the Foreign Office forecast that within a year British trade would have disappeared from Persia altogether.

One apparent solution to this problem was to occupy the south of Persia. British troops could then introduce their own brand of law and order and the roads could be patrolled. Grey shuddered at the thought. The expense would be tremendous and Parliament would never approve. The Government of India had neither men nor money for the exercise and the Foreign Office had no wish to incur any fresh responsibilities in that way. There were a few Indian soldiers stationed at Shiraz but these merely fulfilled the function of guarding British consulates in the south and they were not up to the task of pacifying the region. Furthermore, if the British did move in, in force, on the pretext of protecting their trade then in no time at all Russia would act similarly and inundate the north of Persia with her troops and probably occupy the country right up to the boundary of the British sphere. Such were Grey's apprehensions. In January 1912 the British government decided to withdraw the small Shiraz force rather than to send in reinforcements and to pull back to the coast the consulate staffs and all British subjects inland. Grey wanted stability in Persia but not the responsibility for its imposition. That was a matter for the Persian government, weak as it was, and it was to assist the latter that he directed his attention.

The British government put forward a most unusual compromise. It involved the formation of a Persian gendarmerie under military officers supplied by a neutral foreign power. In this case the gendarmerie was to be commanded by Swedish officers. There were few precedents for such a project — and none at all outside Persia itself. It is more reminiscent of the United Nations than of European diplomacy before the First World War. It resulted directly from the conflict which existed between Britain and Russia in Persia. Britain would never tolerate the use of a Russian officered police force in the south of Persia: Russia, likewise, would never allow the employment of British military officers and officials in the north. Grey arranged for Swedish officers to be imported in order to forestall the possibility of a political deadlock.

The problem of the employment of foreign nationals in the service of the Persian government was not new. Since the late 1890s financial advisers had been drawn from Belgium and France. Morgan Shuster's appointment as Treasurer-General in 1911 was another instance of how the Persians had to look to a neutral western nation for official advisers. His downfall in December 1911 was due largely to his failure to appreciate that fact. Shuster had wished to appoint British subjects as treasury officials in two towns inside the Russian sphere and to appoint a British army officer to command his special treasury gendarmerie, whose area of duties would have extended as far as the Russian frontier. The Russian government reacted violently and Shuster had to be dismissed by the Persians when Russian forces threatened to occupy Tehran.

For the Persian gendarmerie to police the southern roads the Government of India favoured the use of British officers. Grey insisted, though, that the Swedes were less likely to excite Russian sensibilities. Because of its political importance British officials were very anxious that the scheme should work. The Viceroy, Charles Hardinge, reflected in June 1914 that 'our influence in the interior of southern Persia has been on the wane, largely owing to the state of rampant disorder and anarchy that has prevailed on the trade routes by which our trade has been absolutely paralysed'[1]. To the men in London and to the Tehran legation this was perfectly obvious. What was less obvious was the Swedes' achievement. Townley, the British Minister, thought that they had done exceptionally well. The consular staff, however, were less impressed. Townley considered that the Swedes were carrying out a task which was essential to British interests in the south of Persia and that the entire gendarmerie acted as a bulwark against the growing power of Russian consular agents in the neutral sphere. The consular staff could not deny that this was what had been hoped for but they criticised the Swedish commanders for their inefficiency and inexperience. The Foreign Office eventually accepted that the idea had not lived up to expectations. Nicolson questioned Townley's judgement: Hardinge too deemed the gendarmerie to have been a failure.

The fault did not lie with the British government; Grey had done all he could to get the scheme off the ground. He had arranged it with the Persian government and had done his best to try to get the Russian government to allow it to operate in the northern sphere. In January 1913 the British government advanced £100,000 to Persia to enable the Governor-General of the province of Fars to restore order on the trade routes by organizing and equipping the force. But the British could not

1   Memorandum by Hardinge to Cox, 6 June 1914, *Kitchener Papers, Birdwood Collection*, 1906-14, D686/50.

subsidize the gendarmerie indefinitely. When, in March 1914, Townley recommended a further advance of £150,000 to keep it going the Foreign Office had to refuse. Though officials in London admitted that to make the advance would strengthen Britain's position in the southern and central provinces they wanted some indication that an end to such requests for money was in sight. Townley could not provide that: nor could anyone else. Yet if the British government did not continue the gendarmerie what else could it do? Nicolson had no faith in a policy of doling out money to such an inefficient body, but the only alternatives were to send in British troops or to let the south of Persia go altogether and risk the possibility of Russian occupation. In June the Cabinet authorised an advance of £25,000 to keep the gendarmerie operating and the Government of India provided an equivalent sum. Not until November 1914 did the British government 'tire of pouring money into the bottomless pit called the Persian treasury' and finally abandon this novel and, in many respects, most enterprising scheme.[1] By then, of course, the pacification of the south of Persia had sunk low on the list of the British government's priorities.

A further aspect of Lansdowne's policy in the south of Persia had been his protection for the Imperial Bank. Again Grey followed in his path. Support for the Bank was part of maintaining exclusive British liens on the Gulf customs revenues. In a more general sense, however, Grey was also prepared to give the Bank diplomatic assistance at Tehran in settling its grievances with the Persian government and in reclaiming its debts. The Bank was informed in 1907 that His Majesty's Government fully recognised the claim of the Bank to its support.

Had the joint advance with the Russian government after 1906 materialised the Imperial Bank would have acted as the agent for the British government. When the Russian Banque des Prets organized a run on the Imperial Bank in March 1906 the embassy at St Petersburg firmly protested to the Russian government. A year later the Foreign Office discouraged all efforts to form a separate Persian national bank. In November 1910 the Foreign Office agreed that, for the forthcoming loan to Persia, the Bank might state in the prospectus that its agents in Persia would receive diplomatic aid in the performance of their duties when collecting the revenues of the Gulf ports on which the loan was to be secured. This promise was confirmed in June 1911 after the terms of the loan had been settled. Throughout 1910 the British government preferred the Imperial Bank to its competitors. Again the established principle of *laissez-faire* was overruled. In public the British govern-

1   Duboulay to O'Connor, 28 November 1914, *Hardinge Papers*, vol. 88. no. 356.

ment, as always, stressed its impartiality between competing British firms. In the opinion of the Foreign Office, however, 'the Bank was an old established British institution with whom we had worked for years and it was the state bank of Persia. We therefore should naturally prefer that any money lending operations with the Persian government should be conducted by the Bank rather than by any other group'.[1] In 1912, when Baring Brothers were trying to organize a Persian loan in London, the Foreign Office intervened to ensure that the Imperial Bank was duly offered a share in the business. 'We are under far greater obligation to the Imperial Bank than to Messrs. Baring', an Under-Secretary decided. 'When a loan is made to Persia', a colleague confirmed, 'we must not overlook the claim of the Imperial Bank to participate in it'.[2] Grey even tried to persuade the Government of India to continue the subsidy of £1,500 per annum for the Bank's Seistan branch after 1908, though without much success. Although the Viceroy eventually agreed to continue the subsidy it was only on condition that the Bank undertook combined banking and trading agency business, and this its directors were unable to do.

Grey's opportunities for reinforcing Britain's hold on the south of Persia were far greater than those available to his predecessor. During Grey's term of office British concessionaires were active in the region of the Persian Gulf; he therefore had the chance to push these forward in an attempt to extend British interests on the ground. Furthermore, the Russo-Persian agreements of 1890 and 1900 which prohibited railway construction in the country were due to expire in 1910. The time was approaching when railways could be substituted for roads as agents for the spread of trade and for the diffusion of political power.

The concept of railway building for strategic purposes is not one which is normally associated with British policy in the nineteenth or early twentieth centuries. Far more attention has been given to this theme as an aspect of German political and economic expansion in the Middle East and of Russian expansion in Central and Eastern Asia. German railway planning in Asiatic Turkey is well known. A German company first gained the right to construct a stretch of railway in 1889 and ten years later received from the Sultan the initial concession to extend a German line across Mesopotamia, via Bagdad, to the Persian

1   Minute by Maxwell on Seligman Brothers to Foreign Office, 24 October 1910, F.O. 371/958.

2   Minute by Mallet on Errington to Nicolson, 7 December 1912, F.O. 371/1435; and minute by Parker on Buchanan to Grey, 1 December 1912, F.O. 371/1448.

Gulf. The Bagdad railway remained a thorn in the side of British diplomacy in the Middle East until 1914; British officials regarded this, as indeed they did all German economic enterprise in Asia, as being the forerunner of German political claims. The Germans were also eager to build railways in the province of Shantung which they had designated as their special sphere in China in 1897.

Russian railways also had a strategic rationale. The programme of railway construction in Central Asia between 1880 and 1904 had confirmed Russia's hold upon the Khanates and had brought the north of Persia and Afghanistan within the range of military operations. Likewise a trans-Siberian railway had been prominent in the minds of Russian statesmen in the 1890s. It was authorized in 1891 and became a significant feature of Russian policy and diplomacy in the Far East. Again it was the intention of the Russian government to consolidate its authority in newly won territories by means of railways. The Balkan states were the scene of considerable international rivalry over railways in the late nineteenth and early twentieth centuries. Austria, Russia, Turkey and the minor powers all disputed routes and alignments with an eye always on strategic considerations.

Yet any impression that the British lagged behind in respect of strategic railways is not accurate. When British railway activity in Persia is considered it must be borne in mind that the difficulties which British officials faced there were by no means unique. Nowhere were railways more a function of military strategy than on the north-west frontier of India. For years the Indian authorities had tried to prevent railway building which threatened India's inaccessibility by an overland approach. Curzon, as Viceroy, had modified the Government of India's outlook. Under his auspices the British railhead had been pushed forward to Nushki and plans were drawn up for extending a railway up to the frontier positions between Kabul and Kandahar. The tribes of the frontier region could thus be brought more effectively under the control of the Indian army. Troops and supplies could be moved up more quickly if the need arose to defend the mountain passes against a Russian advance. The question of railway construction and frontier defence was one which preoccupied the Indian authorities until 1914. In previous years a Cape to Cairo railway had been dreamt of as a means of unifying Britain's territorial possessions in East Africa, and of thwarting the completion of any French line which might cross the African continent from West to East. Similarly the Foreign Office saw the projection of European railways in China in strategic terms. It tried to stop the most important concessions in China from falling into French, German, or Russian hands and thereby providing the basis for a division of the Chinese empire into spheres of foreign interest.

The same was true in Turkey, though here the British government was far less successful in ensuring that railway development came under its supervision. In the late 1900s the Foreign Office conceived the idea of applying to the Turkish government for a wholly British railway concession to run between Bagdad and the Persian Gulf as one possible means of killing the German Bagdad railway. In 1913-14 considerable efforts were made to protect the one British railway firm which was still operating in Turkey — the Smyrna-Aidin Railway Company. In Persia, officials at the Foreign Office had worked in conjunction with British financiers and railway contractors in the mid 1880s to try to gain a concession for a line from Tehran to the Persian Gulf, and to establish a syndicate in London which would be financially strong enough to undertake the scheme. In 1890 the British Minister at Tehran had argued strongly for a British railway from Baluchistan into Seistan. The strategic value of the line was to the fore: it would greatly strengthen the authority of the Government of India in this south-eastern province of Persia. British railway policy in Persia in the late 1900s must be set against this much wider background of strategic railway planning in the period 1880 to 1914. Only by doing so can the implications of such economic development for political thinking, and vice versa, be fully appreciated.

To some extent the British government had already prepared the way for British railways in the south of Persia. The promise of 1888 from the Shah ensured that if any concession for a railway in the north were given to Russia then a line southwards from Tehran to the Gulf would be granted to a British company, and this pledge was confirmed by the Persian government in 1900. The 1907 Convention meant that any British railway could now only run up to the boundary of the Russian sphere, but otherwise the assurance was unimpaired. It had always been a tenet of Foreign Office policy that 'as soon as Russia built in the north, we should build in the south'.[1] At the same time, though, British officials had been happy to see the general veto imposed on Persian railway construction. At least that had postponed the growth of a Russian railway network over the northern provinces and it thus slowed down the process by which Russia was bringing that region under her control. Lansdowne had concluded at the end of 1903 that 'we shall probably do well to keep alive the Russian embargo as long as we can'[2] — a view which the Indian authorities fully shared. The

1 Memorandum by Mallet, 20 January 1913, F.O. 371/1709.
2 Minute by Lansdowne on Spring-Rice to Lansdowne, 23 November 1903, F.O. 60/678.

Foreign Office had no wish to usher in an age of railway development in Persia unless it was strictly necessary.

Railways in Persia were not just a matter of strategy. The economic background was much discussed, and it was politically important. Railways could divert the flow of trade. They could saturate an area with products hitherto uneconomical to market. If Russia brought her railway system through to the boundary of her sphere in Persia and if the British built no lines in the south, then the trade of the whole of central Persia would be deflected northwards and British goods would be undercut in all the major towns. The same would be true, of course, in reverse. If the British built lines inland from the Gulf, Russian trade in northern Persia would be threatened and her political ascendency reduced. No diplomatic understanding could obscure this basic clash of economic interests in Persia nor its political implications.

The line to which British officials attached the greatest importance and where Russian co-operation would have been welcome was one projected northwards from the Karun River (at Mohammerah) to Khorremabad. It was hoped that the Russians might extend this line northwards from Khorremabad to Hamadan and Julfa inside their sphere. The Russians, however, were unwilling to see this railway built since it would open up the whole of western Persia to British goods entering from the Gulf. Though they did agree to the line in principle they clearly wanted freight rates to be fixed in such a way as to prevent British manufactures from undercutting Russian products in the north of Persia. In 1908 British trade passing from the Gulf northwards to the great distribution centre of Hamadan was valued at over £1 million. To reach that destination it had to be shipped up the Tigris to Bagdad and then carried by caravan eastwards into Persia. A railway northwards from Mohammerah would greatly expand that traffic. It would also divert and multiply British goods destined for Tabriz, worth £150,000 in 1908, which had to be brought overland from the Black Sea port of Trebizond. This was the strictly economic side of the question. In short, the railway would enable British traders to carry the commercial contest in Persia into the Russian sphere — an area which, of late, the Russians had come to look upon as exclusively their own. Politically, the results would be more serious still. The expansion of British trade in western Persia would slow the growth of Russia's political penetration through her banking activities and the actions of her consular agents.

The Mohammerah-Khorremabad railway also became a factor in the defence of Britain's supremacy in the Persian Gulf. By the late 1900s British officials had begun to look upon the project as a possible answer to the Bagdad railway. Ideally the British wanted to take part in the construction of the Bagdad line. If the section southwards from Bagdad to the Persian Gulf were British there would be no danger of a foreign power establishing a foothold on the Gulf littoral nor any obstacle to British trade moving inland. But the Germans would not admit participation by British financiers on terms which the Foreign Office could approve. Until 1914 the British were faced with the prospect of a wholly German railway running through Mesopotamia to the Gulf. This involved a distinct threat to British trade. If the Germans fixed the freight rates on their railway so as to discriminate against British manufactures then British goods trying to enter the north of Persia from the Gulf would be unable to compete with German manufactures coming overland by rail. A British railway from Mohammerah to Khorremabad could pre-empt that problem. British trade would be able to move directly northwards from the Persian Gulf. Moreover, Britain's bargaining power for a share in the Bagdad railway would be greatly strengthened. After 1905 the Foreign Office accepted the view that 'it will be those who first build and control the railways that abut on the Persian Gulf who will hold the key to the whole position'.[1]

Having settled these matters in their minds the British next had to tackle the practical issues. How was the railway to be financed? How was the concession to be obtained from the Persian government? How was Russian opposition to the project to be overcome? It was certain that no private capital would be forthcoming for railway construction while Persia, and particularly the south, remained in a state of chaos. Only a British government guarantee could goad investors to put their money into Persian railways but a guarantee was out of the question. True, the Treasury had provided funds for Persia in 1903 and 1904 contrary to former practice, but when it came to guaranteeing economic enterprise abroad the resistance to any change of attitude was still strong. Similarly, the Treasury would not contemplate a direct subsidy. In that respect the rules which governed the use of public revenues were much the same as they had been in the early 1900s when Lansdowne had been forced to raid secret service funds for money with which to encourage Persian roads. Furthermore, both the Persian and Russian governments had declared their opposition to the Mohammerah – Khorremabad project. However to the British it did not matter that they could not start to build the line so long as the Germans showed no signs of completing the Bagdad railway and so long as the Russians made no move to begin railway construction in the north. All that the

1   Memorandum by Elliot, 22 September 1905, F.O. 60/707.

Foreign Office wanted for the time being was the option for the line.

Apart from the Mohammerah-Khorremabad line the British government wanted options for railways from Kerman to Bunder Abbas, from Bunder Abbas via Shiraz to Ahwaz, and from Bushire to a point on the Bunder Abbas-Ahwaz route. To gain all these would be effectively to seal off the south of Persia from the possibility of non-British railway construction. The dangers of not doing so were obvious. 'If foreigners invest capital they will acquire claims which their governments will utilize to gain political influence and back by diplomacy or even by arms', the Foreign Office was reminded. 'Such a state of affairs will embarrass and prejudice our position in India'.[1] With respect to the last of these alignments, Grey persuaded the Treasury in December 1909 to pay half the cost for a surveying party. The Foreign Office impressed upon the Chancellor of the Exchequer 'that the results of the operation proposed would be of the greatest use and profit'.[2] Since the veto on railway construction in Persia was due to expire in a few months time, and since the Bagdad railway seemed to be advancing gradually towards the Persian Gulf, decisions were needed about British railway policy in the south. In the interim the Foreign Office pursued a 'blocking policy'[3] — though even this implication that railways might be built in Persia in the future was almost too much for the India Office. 'It comes therefore to this', the Political Secretary at the India Office remarked. 'Russia wants railways in Persia for commercial and political reasons. We do not want them for commercial and political reasons. Neither of us has money to build them at present. The Persian government do not want to grant concessions. Our immediate purpose is only to keep the Germans out. What is really *our* interest is to keep railways out of Persia altogether for another ten years'.[4] Nicolson, at the Foreign Office, replied that the British government was not committed to build a railway merely because it had secured an option. 'We need only earmark them and postpone construction for a lengthy period'.[5]

This attitude changed somewhat after 1910 when it became clear that the Russians would press ahead with railway construction down to the boundary of their sphere and that some corresponding initiative was

1   *Ibid.*

2   Foreign Office to Treasury, 1 December 1909, F.O. 371/719.

3   Hardinge to Nicolson, 30 September 1908, *Nicolson Papers,* F.O. 800/341.

4   Memorandum by Hirtzel, 21 December 1909, I.O. L/P&S/10/160, 1908; and minute by Hirtzel on Cox to India Office, 25 July 1911, I.O. L/P&S/10/177, file: 18.

5   Nicolson to Morley, 24 December 1909, *Morley Papers,* D573/49.

necessary in the south. Even the India Office sensed that times had changed; Russian and German railways in Persia were now regarded as inevitable. 'The geographical isolation of India is necessarily doomed', the India Office concluded in April 1911. 'It behoves those who are responsible for her interests to be foremost in the race for concessions, so as to ensure that such at least as may be strategically and politically essential shall be in her own hands'.[1] The Foreign Office agreed that Britain could no longer abstain from railway construction. Without railways northwards from the Gulf British trade would lose its pre-eminence in the markets of southern and central Persia, 'and with it would disappear our influence'.[2] Barclay and the Foreign Office discussed the possibility of persuading private financial houses to apply for a concession for the Mohammerah-Khorremabad railway. In 1913 the India Office emphasised that the construction of railways was 'the only means likely to be effective in the long run of maintaining British influence in a region where its maintenance is essential to the security of India'.[3] In fact the Foreign Office had long recognised this. Even before the India Office changed its tune on railway matters the Foreign Office had taken steps to try to overcome the reluctance of both the Russian and Persian governments to approve the Mohammerah-Khorremabad scheme.

Representations to the Russian government were singularly unrewarding. Sazanoff, the Russian Foreign Minister, saw any railway from the head of the Persian Gulf northwards towards the Russian sphere as a threat to Russian commerce. He was not at all disposed to help British traders all the more by building a Russian line down from Julfa to form an extension. The value of the Mohammerah-Khorremabad railway as a check upon the German Bagdad railway appealed to him a little more, but not enough to allay his basic fear for Russian trade and influence in the north of Persia. Russia could not prevent a British firm from building a railway up to the boundary of the Russian sphere. The line would run through the neutral zone in Persia and Russia was therefore bound by the 1907 Convention not to oppose it. All the same, if the Foreign Office wished to preserve the spirit of that Convention it would have to think twice before pressing ahead with a project to which it was known Russian statesmen took exception. The Russian government argued that Moscow merchants objected to the line since it

1   India Office to Foreign Office, 6 April 1911, enclosed with papers of the sub-committee of the Committee for Imperial Defence in Hankey to Parker, 12 April 1913, F.O. 371/1711.

2   Memorandum by Mallet, 20 January 1913, F.O. 371/1709.

3   India Office to Foreign Office, 1 April 1913, F.O. 371/1711.

would mean that British sea-borne goods could be brought up to Hamadan from the Gulf by rail at a lower price than Russian products coming overland. Grey replied that if the Mohammerah railway were not built then with the advent of the Bagdad railway British trade would be pushed out of northern and central Persia altogether. By the Potsdam agreement between Russia and Germany of 1911 Russia had made provision for the entry of German goods into northern Persia by rail. Why therefore did the Russian government wish to discriminate against British manufactures?

No satisfactory answer was forthcoming. In March 1911 the Russian government made some concession to Britain when it agreed not to object to her simply earmarking the line. Then the Russians threw out hints about British capital being used to help in the development of Russian railways in the north: but the Foreign Office only replied that that was a matter for private British financiers and not one in which the British government could interfere. In the meantime Grey was growing very impatient with the lack of co-operation from St Petersburg – the more so since it reflected badly on his policy as seen from home. 'It becomes increasingly desirable to show public opinion here that Anglo-Russian co-operation leads to something more than occupation of places in Persia by Russian troops', he telegraphed to Townley. 'For this purpose it would be most valuable if the concession for the Mohammerah-Khorremabad railway could be put through'.[1] Not until September 1912 did Sazanoff finally withdraw his opposition to the construction of the Mohammerah-Khorremabad railway. The Russians, however, were only one party to the necessary arrangements. While trying to convince Sazanoff of the need for the Mohammerah line Grey had also had to try to win the favour of the Persian government.

In Tehran the Majlis opposed the concession on two accounts. First, it disliked the prospect of any further foreign economic initiatives in Persia. Secondly, to grant a concession for a railway from the Gulf which stopped short at the boundary of the Russian sphere was, in effect, to recognize the validity of the 1907 Convention and to acknowledge that the country was divided into zones of foreign influence. Hitherto no Persian government had recognized the Anglo-Russian agreement. Even Mohammed Ali Shah had refused to admit that his kingdom was divided. There was little chance, therefore, that the constitutionalist party would do so. It seemed that the Mohammerah-Khorremabad railway would fall foul of the growth of Persian nationalism which had taken place in the mid 1900s.

1 Grey to Townley, 22 October 1912, F.O. 371/1448.

In May 1911 the Foreign Office realized that negotiations with Persia had reached an impasse. The railway, for the Persians too, was charged with political implications. The best the Foreign Office could do was to try to find a private company which might approach the Persian government and lay the scheme before it as a purely commercial proposition. Any attempt by the Tehran legation to assist would immediately wreck all chances of success. With the disappearance of the Majlis in December 1911, though, things began to change. By July 1912 Townley was planning to get the Mohammerah-Khorremabad concession 'by the use of moral pressure'. 'Should this fail', he wrote to Grey, 'more drastic measures of persuasion could be resorted to'. But the Persians still proved inflexible. The Foreign Office was most angry when the Russians were granted a concession actually to build a railway from Julfa to Tabriz in February 1913 while there was still no sign even of an option being given for the Mohammerah line. This inequality of treatment was most regrettable, Grey remarked. He would tolerate no further delay in granting the necessary option to the British company which had applied.

The company in question was the Persian Railways Syndicate. This was a strong financial group which was formed by British oil interests in Persia, the Imperial Bank of Persia, the Persian Transport Company, Indian shipping interests, and investment trusts in London. Its directorate comprised the representatives of all these concerns. In addition, the Persian Railways Syndicate was associated with important British mining rights in the province of Kerman. The Foreign Office willingly supported such a group; this was plainly no speculative venture but an association of some of the most substantial British investments in the Middle East. Grey's insistence on the Syndicate's behalf had some effect. It received the right to survey a route from Mohammerah to Khorremabad and an option on construction to run for two years. The most important line in southern Persia had thereby been secured for British contractors.

The British government's resolution to earmark railway concessions had inevitably led to its involvement with the financiers who were interested in them. Although the Foreign Office had done nothing to press the Mohammerah-Khorremabad project while the Majlis was in session, after its dissolution Townley felt no impediment to giving the Persian Railways Syndicate all the help that he could muster. More than that, the Foreign Office decided the form which the company's

1   Townley to Grey, 25 July 1912, F.O. 371/1434.

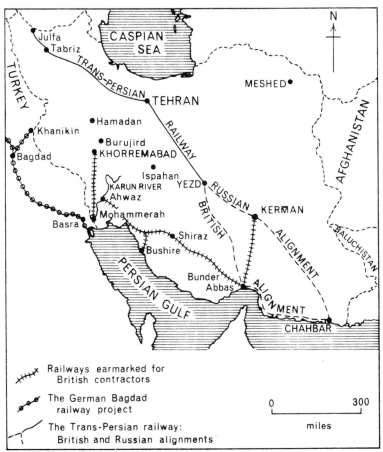

Map 3 FOREIGN RAILWAY PROJECTS IN PERSIA 1910–1914

application should take. In July 1911 the Syndicate was advised as to the best gauge for railways in the south, exactly which concessions should be applied for, and what the security for any money lent to the Persian government should be. When the Syndicate was preparing to apply for the Mohammerah line in April 1912 the Foreign Office had no hesitation in supplying direction. In fact the Foreign Office had been a guiding spirit in the formation of the company itself in 1911. It had been eager for the major firms concerned with southern Persia to form a combination for the purpose of railway building, and it had done its best to smooth over the differences of opinion which arose between the various parties. The Persian Railways Syndicate was one of the instruments with which the British government staked out its claim to paramountcy in the south of Persia. Its role thus resembled that of the Persian Transport Company in respect of road building back in 1904. By the end of 1912 the Foreign Office privately acknowledged that the Syndicate would be given preference over any competitors.

The Mohammerah-Khorremabad line and the other railways planned for southern Persia were only one aspect of the British government's attempt to determine the pattern of railway construction. Equally important was the approach which it adopted to the proposal that Britain and Russia should co-operate to build a trunk line across the country to connect the Russian and Indian railway networks.

This trans-Persian venture had not been conceived in London. The Indian authorities regarded it with extreme suspicion. 'The whole talk of a land route to India has been of a piece with that damned sentimental folly of the Cape to Cairo railway', the Secretary of State wrote to the Viceroy in 1913.[1] The High Command in India was resolutely opposed to the idea. 'There can be very little doubt that nobody likes the proposal', the India Office wrote in 1913, 'and that everybody would gladly see it dropped'.[2] A railway right across Persia was the thing that British and Indian officials dreaded above all else. The Viceroy wrote home in 1909 that 'wide tracts of country without railways still remaining outside our frontier constitute most important factors in the defence of India'.[3] The project would completely undermine the value of Persia as a buffer state.

The initiative for a trans-Persian railway, needless to say, had come from Russia. It would be, the Russians claimed, an indication of the new spirit of Anglo-Russian co-operation. Surely having signed the 1907 Convention the British did not still harbour suspicions as to Russia's friendly intentions? Grey's position was most awkward: the Indian authorities and influential opinion in London retained the strongest doubts as to the wisdom of the Convention in the first place. Nonetheless, Grey wished to preserve the *entente* with Russia. It was important, therefore, that no offence should be given. 'If we decide that the whole thing must be discouraged and opposed, the effect will be very chilling', he informed the India Office in 1910.[4] The Germans

1   Crewe to Hardinge, 17 January 1913, *Hardinge Papers,* vol. 75.

2   Memorandum by Hirtzel enclosed in India Office to Foreign Office, 6 January 1913, F.O. 371/1709.

3   Minto to Morley, 11 November 1909, *Morley Papers,* D573/22.

4   Grey to Crewe, 25 November 1911, *Grey Papers,* F.O. 800/98.

had apparently convinced the Tsar that the trans-Persian railway was an important test case for the spirit of Anglo-Russian co-operation. To decline all Russian overtures might drive the Russian government into some agreement with Germany for the development of railways in the Middle East and this might prove far more dangerous for the British.

The British government's agreement to consider the project was therefore conditioned largely by the wish to keep on good terms with Russia and to preserve the wider understanding in Europe. Clearly there were those in London, and even more so in India, who thought that the trans-Persian would be no less a tool of Russian expansion than the trans-Caspian or trans-Siberian railways had been. Grey decided, however, that the risk had to be taken. The Foreign Office observed in 1912 that 'we cannot afford to quarrel with Russia over this, now that it is taking shape, especially as she is going to spend so many millions on her fleet'.[1] The policy of trying to 'sterilize' Persia as far as railway development was concerned was superficially abandoned. In September 1912 Townley was asked to join with his Russian colleague at Tehran in pressing the Persian government for an option for the trans-Persian line, at least as far as the limit of the Russian sphere.

There were other reasons why it was better to join with the Russians in a trans-Persian railway than to reject the proposal out of hand. By co-operating with Russia the British government would have a say in the way in which the scheme developed. If Russian overtures were dismissed outright there was little doubt that Russia would turn her attention to developing her own lines in the northern and neutral spheres of Persia, soon Britain would be confronted with Russian and possibly even German lines extending as far south as Yezd and Ispahan and as far east as Kerman on the boundary of the British sphere. 'Politically', the Committee of Imperial Defence reported, 'the result of this would be the disappearance of British influence in Persia'.[2] To fail to keep the spirit of co-operation with Russia in Persia alive, Nicolson concluded, 'would work to our detriment, both politically and commercially'.[3] It was also argued that a through railway from Europe to India was inevitable. What was more, Britain had to hold out some inducement in order to gain Russian assent to the Mohammerah-Khorremabad railway.

---

1   Minute by Mallet with respect to articles in *The Times* of 14 and 15 June 1912, F.O. 371/1434.

2   Draft report of the sub-committee of the Committee for Imperial Defence, in Hankey to Parker, 12 April 1913, F.O. 371/1711.

3   Nicolson to Townley, 7 April 1914, *Nicolson Papers*, F.O. 800/373.

The British remained double-faced in respect of the trans-Persian railway. Grey, despite his professions of friendship for Russia, had no wish to see the line built. He took the view that 'nothing but trouble, mischief, and danger can come to the Government of India from any of these approaches to India from Europe'.[1] The British dragged their feet over the whole business from its first serious suggestion in 1909 until the outbreak of war in 1914. No-one at the Foreign Office believed the line to be a practicable proposition. After the British government had decided that it was best served by accommodating Russian wishes, an official observed that it was no doubt safe to do so because the chances of the railway actually being constructed were very remote. The Ambassador in St Petersburg assured Grey in 1914 that this was still the case. Nicolson too believed that a long period of time would be needed before the railway 'would come into the field of practical politics'.[2] The Foreign Office was also aware that it could kill the plan at any time if strategic considerations made it necessary to do so. When the question of a British government guarantee was raised and flatly refused in 1911, the Foreign Office speculated there and then that a deathblow had probably been dealt to the whole idea. 'Should we eventually find that it is opposed to our interests', the Ambassador wrote from Russia in 1912, 'it will not be difficult for us to find some way of obstructing it indirectly when the financial side of the question comes up for discussion'.[3]

In the meantime the Foreign Office contented itself with endless discussion about the possible alignment of the trans-Persian railway and the point where the Russian and Indian gauges should meet. Within a few months it had succeeded in modifying the scheme out of all recognition, and it had frustrated the attempts of the Russian government and of the British financial group involved to begin any surveying work or to draw up plans. The question of alignment was obviously of the greatest strategic importance. The Russians wanted the line to run from Tehran to Yezd and then to run eastwards, entering the British sphere at Kerman and striking the coast at the port of Chahbar. The British agreed as far as Yezd, but they claimed that the line should run south-east to meet the coast at Bunder Abbas and to follow it along towards the Indian frontier. The Kerman alignment was out of the question as far as the Government of India was concerned. The General Staff calculated that in the event of an Anglo-Russian war any trans-

1   Minute by Grey on Buchanan to Grey, 18 April 1911, F.O. 371/1178.
2   Nicolson to Hardinge, 12 January 1910, *Hardinge Papers,* vol. 20.
3   Buchanan to Grey, 22 July 1912, F.O. 371/1434.

Persian line would allow Russia to concentrate about 200,000 men on the frontier of the British sphere in Persia within the space of four months; if the railway ran far from the coast Britain would be powerless to resist this build-up of forces. If the railway struck the coast at Bunder Abbas, however, and if it followed the coast thereafter, then the line would be exposed to naval attack from the Indian Ocean and Russia would be forced to tie down half her invading army simply defending her line of communication.

The break of gauge on the railway between the Russian and Indian systems was likewise a controversial issue. This was a question of controlling the rolling stock in the event of war. If the gauge changed at a point from which the British would have to retire immediately hostilities began, all the rolling stock to the south of that point would easily fall into Russian hands and would be used to hasten her advance through the British sphere. Ideally the gauge should change at a point on the line which British forces could hold for long enough to allow the rolling stock to be taken back towards India. Russia's advance would then be considerably slower since her wider-gauge rolling stock could only be used as and when a third rail was laid alongside the existing track.[1] In February 1913 the Foreign Office informed the British company involved in the project of the conditions on which it would allow discussions about the railway to continue. The line could not be extended outside the Russian sphere until the British government considered it politic to do so. Bunder Abbas had to be the point at which it met the coast. When that stage was reached the British government would decide whether the line could be extended farther.

Here again the Foreign Office was supervising very closely the activities of British financiers. A railway through Persia was far too important a matter to be left free from official direction. Strategy required that the railway should be postponed for as long as possible — not that bankers should relish its construction in the hope of early profits. The trans-Persian railway provides a fine example of how the British clung to their traditional policy in Persia: the isolation of India from Europe overland was not to be surrendered lightly. Only to the west of Bunder Abbas were the British prepared to see railways built: principally this was in the area around the Karun River. Even here, though, blocking options sufficed. Although the British realised by

---

[1] Memorandum by the chief of the Indian General Staff, 5 September 1912, enclosed in Government of India to India Office, 13 February 1913, I.O. L/P&S/10/379, 1913, file: 782; Beauchamp-Duff to Hirtzel, 9 December 1913, I.O. L/P&S/10/416, 1913, file: 4822; and memorandum by Beauchamp-Duff to Ritchie, 2 November 1911, I.O. L/P&S/10/160, 1908, file: 1717.

1912 that Persia could not be propped up for much longer as an independent country they still had faith in their ability to preserve their economic base and their political authority in the area which bordered on the Persian Gulf. Grey's policy was thus an extension of the 'Karun enterprise' into which the Foreign Office had entered so enthusiastically in the early 1900s.

This general policy did not rely entirely upon railways. Any economic enterprise in the south of Persia would strengthen Britain in the area and the government therefore took an active interest in all British undertakings. The late 1900s saw greater opportunities for capital investment in southern Persia. First, because important mineral resources had been discovered there, the exploitation of which offered greater rewards than the construction of roads had done in previous years. Secondly, because economic enterprise near the Gulf derived some security from the knowledge that British naval protection was always near at hand. A few important British firms began to operate in the south of Persia before 1914 and all of them came to work closely with officials in London or with the legation at Tehran.

Oil was foremost among British investments in the south. By 1914 it dominated economic activity there to an extent which had seemed impossible ten years before. The oil industry in Persia dated from the time of the petroleum concession to Knox D'Arcy in May 1901. This initial concession ran for 60 years and it gave D'Arcy the right of exploration, of exploitation, and of exporting oil from all of Persia save the five northern provinces. In return D'Arcy had paid £20,000 in cash to the Persian government, he had promised a further £20,000 in shares of any company formed, and he had agreed to pay the Persian government a royalty of 16 per cent of annual profits. An exploration company was formed in 1903 with an initial capital of £400,000.

D'Arcy's search, alas, was unrewarded. By 1905 his exploration company was running short of money and he was not inclined to sink any more into what was proving an unsuccessful speculation. Without assistance from outside the exploration company seemed doomed to failure. At this point the British government stepped in. The Admiralty had been considering the question of energy supplies for the navy and it had decided that oil would gradually replace coal as the major fuel. Oil supply thus became a matter of strategic importance. The Admiralty had to guard against the danger of needing to buy oil at monopoly prices and it had to ensure that the source of supply was an area subject to British control. The Persian Gulf was such an area and the British government decided that the search for oil there should be continued.

To achieve that end the Admiralty persuaded Lord Strathcona and his Glasgow firm (the Burmah Oil Company) to go to D'Arcy's rescue.

Burmah Oil brought in new capital. It took over the original concession and it began new explorations under the auspices of the Concessions Syndicate Limited. But it could not find oil. By April 1908, much to the disappointment of the British government, the Syndicate had decided to withdraw from Persia. Instructions were issued: then, at the very last moment, a large strike was made. From then on the future of British oil was assured. In April 1909 the Anglo-Persian Oil Company was launched, its chief shareholders being Burmah Oil, the Concessions Syndicate, and Lord Strathcona. The stock and ordinary shares which were issued to the public were taken up within half an hour. The Anglo-Persian Oil Company's capital was £2 million. In 1912 its refinery was completed on the island of Abadan which, two years later, was exporting refined oil at the rate of a quarter of a million tons per annum. To safeguard the Admiralty's source of supply the British government, in 1914, raised the total capital of the Company to over £4 million, thereby acquiring a controlling interest and the right to appoint two directors.[1]

The discovery of oil obviously had an importance beyond simply safeguarding Britain's political authority in the south of Persia. Yet officials at the Foreign Office did not neglect this aspect of the oil industry nor underestimate its significance for their policy of economic penetration there. On the occasion of the first major oil strike in May 1908 Charles Hardinge pointed out that it was 'excellent news for our interests in south-west Persia'.[2] An official observed that the oil company 'gives British interests an increased stake in the Bakhtiari country'.[3] 'This discovery of oil should bring prosperity to the region', Hardinge replied, 'and greatly increase our interest in south-western Persia'.[4] The Foreign Office thought of asking the Board of Trade to devise some scheme for enticing more British firms to develop oil deposits in the south of Persia. By 1908 such opportunities seemed to

1 For a history of British oil enterprise in Persia in these years see L.P. Elwell-Sutton, *Persian Oil: a study in Power Politics* (London 1955), pp. 10-25. Platt, pp. 239-42. A more detailed study of the Admiralty's interest in Persian Oil is M. Jack, 'The Purchase of the British Government's shares in the British Petroleum Company 1912-14', *Past and Present* (1968).

2 Minute by Hardinge on Marling to Grey, 29 May 1908, F.O. 371/497.

3 Minute by Norman on India Office to Foreign Office, 22 July 1908, F.O. 371/503.

4 Minute by Hardinge on India Office to Foreign Office, 27 July 1908, F.O. 371/497.

be considerable and there was growing apprehension that German concessionaires would realize this. The Foreign Office wrote to the Anglo-Persian Oil Company in September, enclosing reports by the vice-consul at Ahwaz as to the areas into which the Company's operations could profitably be extended. 'From the point of view of British interests, both political and commercial', the letter concluded, it was most desirable that new oil workings should be undertaken by the British firm. Otherwise, it added, the business might be secured by subjects of a foreign power.[1] In 1910 the Foreign Office wanted the Company to make a loan to the Persian government which would effectively purchase the latter's holding in oil exploration and so gain the entire concession for the British group. The Company was less keen on the transaction. 'They are only lending at all to oblige us', an official remarked in August.[2] Clearly the Foreign Office regarded the business in strictly political terms. When, in 1913, negotiations were under way for the absorption of the Anglo-Persian Oil Company by the larger Shell group the British government wished to preserve the former's independent status. The Foreign Office feared that the Shell group would introduce a foreign element into the operations of the oil industry in the south of Persia. Winston Churchill, at the Admiralty, underlined the point. He reminded the Cabinet that 'there are also considerable political interests at stake in the Gulf region'.[3] The India Office confirmed that 'we don't want oil deposits in the British sphere in Persia to pass into foreign hands'.[4] The British government preferred to see an independent British subsidiary company working oil deposits in the region.

After the early 1900s, therefore, the British government was closely involved with the fortunes of British oil. The oil company remained a private venture until 1914. The Foreign Office took no responsibility for the success of its operations. 'We are in no way responsible for the proceedings of the Company which is a private concern entirely beyond our control', the India Office was informed. 'The public must invest or not as they please, judging by the merits of the enterprise'.[5] Yet a moral obligation to support the oil syndicate had been incurred when the Admiralty asked Burmah Oil to rescue the concession in 1905.

1   Foreign Office to D'Arcy, 12 September 1908, F.O. 371/497.

2   Minute by Norman on Barclay to Grey, 24 August 1910, F.O. 371/960.

3   Memorandum by Churchill, July 1913, Cabinet memoranda 1905-18, F.O. 899/1 no. 187.

4   Hirtzel to Maxwell, 3 April 1913, F.O. 371/1728.

5   Maxwell to Ritchie, 5 August 1909, F.O. 371/717.

Moreover, its importance, both to the Admiralty and in respect of policy in southern Persia, meant that official aid would not be denied. The Foreign Office conceded privately in 1909 that it was under an obligation to uphold the oil company in the transaction of its business in Persia.

The legation at Tehran frequently represented the Company's interests to the Persian government. Consular agents also watched over its fortunes. By the late 1900s the Foreign Office had become attentive to the firm's requirements as well. Spring-Rice complained in September 1907 that disorders in the south of Persia jeopardised the future of the oil industry there and made its withdrawal a serious possibility. If that occurred, he warned, 'a probably fatal blow would be struck at British prestige, for whatever be the ostensible reason for withdrawal, the tribesmen and chiefs will ascribe it to no other motive than fear'.[1] In November a small force of 22 men was sent up to Ahwaz to guard the oil company's installations. It remained there for nearly two years. In January 1909 the Company again required the assistance of the Foreign Office. Its promoter wanted Lord Milner to join the board as Chairman and asked if the Foreign Office could arrange the necessary introduction. 'We are unable to do this as it would look like official intervention', Charles Hardinge decided; but the end was achieved by asking if Lord Lansdowne, a personal friend of Milner, would oblige.[2]

Roads also remained politically important, although less so than in the early 1900s. With the prospect of railway construction in the near future roads were now of secondary consideration; the concern of the Foreign Office was to organise a gendarmerie to patrol them. The prevailing disorder made the completion of unfinished roads quite impossible. The Ahwaz-Tehran trunk road, for instance, had been built only to the north of Sultanabad by 1910. Even so, the Foreign Office did not desert the Persian Transport Company – its agent for road construction in Persia. The legation told the Persian government that H.M.G. expected the road concession to be extended beyond the expiry date of 1912 since the Company's inability to fulfil its contract was due to no fault of its own. The Foreign Office retained the right to appoint a director to the board of the Persian Transport Company. It exercised this right in 1912 when its original nominee, who had served on the board since the Company's foundation in 1904, retired. When the latter called at the Foreign Office in 1910 to discuss the question of

1 Spring-Rice to Grey, 13 September 1907, F.O. 371/306.
2 Hardinge to Lansdowne, 4 January 1909, *Hardinge Papers,* vol. 17.

roads and trade routes in Persia it was as the representative of a group which still had a political role to play. An official assumed, quite naturally, that 'we are glad to help him in any way we can'.[1] Despite the difficulties which plagued road construction the process of acquiring concessions remained a matter for official concern. When a British company proposed to tender for the right to build a motor road between Bunder Abbas and Kerman in 1909 the Foreign Office had no hesitation in backing it. The syndicate in question was a strong one, and the scheme itself 'is one which I think that from a political and commercial point of view we should encourage' Hardinge decided.[2] As with railway concessions the essential thing was to stop such important assets from falling into unfriendly hands.

The same applied to telegraph lines. When in 1908 the Treasury refused to allow public funds to be used to purchase the line between Ahwaz and Borasjun from the Persian government the Foreign Office feared that the Germans would step in to buy it. An Under-Secretary observed that the telegraph concession might be of immense importance in determining the allocation of railway enterprise in the area in future years. 'It therefore seems to me a great political interest to us to secure this line', he decided. If the Treasury could be persuaded to put up half the cost the Government of India was almost certain to meet the rest. Charles Hardinge fully agreed. If the line fell under German management, he replied, 'our position in southern Persia would be gravely affected'.[3] In August 1908 Grey informed the Treasury officially that he much regretted their negative decision. Prior to that he had already written privately to the Chancellor of the Exchequer, Lloyd George. 'The acquisition of the control of the line is of the highest political moment', Grey explained, 'and failure to acquire it, with as little delay as possible, whereby the field would be left clear to foreign enterprise, would be most unfortunate'.[4]

Mining concessions offered a further opportunity for the Foreign Office. After 1912 a British firm (the Kerman Mining Company) was interested in a concession for mineral exploitation in the neutral sphere and the legation was instructed to give all the help it could. The

1 Minute by Norman on Lorrimer to Foreign Office, 28 July 1910, F.O. 371/957.

2 Minute by Hardinge on Indo-European Telegraph Company to Foreign Office, 1 October 1909, F.O. 371/714.

3 Minutes by Mallet and Hardinge on Treasury to Foreign Office, 1 April 1908, F.O. 371/501.

4 Foreign Office to Treasury, 11 August 1908, F.O. 371/501.

Kerman Mining Company was a sound venture, linked through its directorate to the Anglo-Persian Oil Company and to the Persian Railways Syndicate. Moreover the mineral rights which it held were known to be extremely valuable. As with the Anglo-Persian Oil Company, the Foreign Office believed that the Kerman Mining Company should remain a distinctly British undertaking. In neither case would the British government welcome shares passing into Russian or German hands. In 1913, when the Russian government began to insist that its nationals should be allowed to participate in the mining business, the Foreign Office found itself in the familiar predicament of trying to remain on good terms with Russia while defending reputable British investments. Ideally co-operation between British and Russians was the solution, on terms which the Kerman group would consider to be satisfactory. After December 1913 the Foreign Office did its best to achieve that end. The fact, though, that the projected alignment for the trans-Persian railway was to pass through the area of the British company's concession provided a further complication, and made any settlement for the Kerman Mining Company dependent on the progress of that larger scheme.

The littoral of the Persian Gulf was also the scene of mineral exploitation. Once more there was concern that German finance might establish a foothold in the area and provide the basis for some political claim. Much to the relief of officials in London, a concession granting a German group the right to work red oxide of iron at Abu Musa was cancelled in July 1907. Three months later a British firm, Messrs. Ellinger and Company, expressed its interest in similar deposits on Hormuz island. Ellinger asked for certain assurances from the British government without which, it was asserted, public subscriptions could not be raised. Grey wished to help the firm, even though by the standards of British oil and railway business it was very small. He urged the India Office to agree that such assurances be given. In December Ellinger felt able to refer to 'the special interests' which the Foreign Office had in seeing the oxide scheme successfully carried through.[1] In January 1908 the Foreign Office promised Ellinger that its concession rights would be protected by the Tehran legation and by the consul at Bunder Abbas, provided that the company remained exclusively British.

Ellinger, however, had a strong competitor in the business. Messrs. Strick and Company was also intent on exploiting red oxide deposits

---

[1] Messrs. Ellinger & Company to Foreign Office, 20 December 1907, F.O. 371/310.

in the Gulf. Strick & Co. was a perfectly respectable group which had a small stake in the Anglo-Persian Oil Company. From the viewpoint of the Foreign Office it mattered little which of the two British companies actually got the concession. A clerk remarked in July 1908: 'I do not think it really matters whether we support Strick or Ellinger so long as we keep out the Germans'.[1] As time passed, however, the Foreign Office came to realise that Strick & Co. was more likely to carry out the business satisfactorily. Strick was thus the man for the Foreign Office: he would do more for Britain's political presence in the region. But Ellinger could not just be thrown over. Such commitments as the British government had given were to Ellinger & Co. by virtue of the declaration of January 1908. The solution was obviously co-operation between these rivals; in fact, the Foreign Office had favoured that idea from the beginning. After July 1908 Grey did his best to bring the two firms together in order to produce a strong British syndicate which would work the oxide deposits. The Foreign Office interviewed their respective representatives and it wrote to the firms explaining the benefits to be gained from collaboration. Five years later, though, they were still at odds. Grey never achieved the formation of a powerful combine to work the oxide: but at least no Germans had managed to gain a concession for its exploitation, and to that extent the Foreign Office had cause for satisfaction. This policy of blocking all non-British concessions in the Persian Gulf was also evident in respect of sulphur deposits near Lingah. Both Ellinger and Strick wanted the concession; again the Foreign Office had no wish to differentiate between competing British interests. However it was determined that the Germans should be excluded. The Foreign Office admitted in June 1913 that 'we have done our best to encourage British firms to apply'.[2]

Irrigation works on the Karun River provided another opening. The Foreign Office believed that any scheme should be undertaken by British contractors and not by those of any other foreign power. The question of lending money to the Persian government with which to finance irrigation was therefore important. The Government of India feared that German capitalists might find the necessary funds, in which case 'Germany will acquire influence over the eastern shore of the Shatt-el-Arab and over the whole of Mohammerah'.[3]

More specifically the threat came from the Dutch. In 1906 Dutch

1 Minute by Norman on Marling to Grey, 19 July 1908, F.O. 371/498.

2 Minute by Norman on Townley to Grey, 20 June 1913, F.O. 371/1718.

3 Government of India to India Office, 23 September 1906, enclosed in India Office to Foreign Office, 26 September 1906, F.O. 371/111.

engineers drew up plans for extensive irrigation works which Grey feared might be accepted by the Persian government. He explained the danger to the Minister at the Hague. In an unsettled country such as Persia even what appeared to be purely commercial undertakings often required foreign protection 'and led to a danger of political interference which might be prejudicial to Persian independence'.[1] Grey succeeded in preventing the Dutch government from giving any encouragement to the project. In 1909 the Foreign Office seemed to think that Dutch enterprise on the Karun might create an opening for the Germans in south-west Persia. Barclay summed up the anxiety which all British officials concerned with Persia felt at the time: it was, he remarked, a 'critical moment in our struggle against German influence in the Persian Gulf'.[2] In April 1909 government departments in London were debating the possibility of finding British firms to invest in the project. It was generally taken for granted that 'the control of the Karun irrigation by British capital is an important factor in regard to our position in the Gulf'.[3]

Grey was also concerned for the fortunes of British trade generally. The wide distribution of British products was the most obvious way to emphasise Britain's claim to ascendency in the south of Persia. In the late 1900s British officials viewed with increasing apprehension the development of German shipping and trade in the Gulf. In May 1914 Nicolson expressed his uneasiness that in the past year the Germans had succeeded in capturing practically the whole of the trade on the Karun River. Before long, he wrote to the embassy at Berlin, they would demand to be consulted on questions relating to Persia and the Gulf. 'In fact', he concluded, 'it will be Morocco over again'.[4] Six years earlier the Viceroy of India had sounded a similar alarm. German trade in the Gulf was already increasing and the completion of the Bagdad railway to the Gulf coast by the Germans was a real threat. Trade meant political authority he reminded the India Office. 'We must remember the huge influence of British prestige. I am not quite sure if you will like my word "prestige",' he reflected, 'but it has a solid value in the East'.[5] The British government, however, seemed to be less worried. When the Karun subsidy for the Euphrates and Tigris Steam Navigation Company came up for renewal at the end of 1906 the

1   Grey to Howard, 12 December 1906, F.O. 371/111.
2   Barclay to Grey, 7 April 1909, F.O. 371/715.
3   Askers to Mallet, 9 April 1909, F.O. 371/713.
4   Nicolson to Goschen, 18 May 1914, *Nicolson Papers*, F.O. 800/374.
5   Minto to Morley, 23 March 1908, *Morley Papers*, D573/14.

Foreign Office was reluctant to continue it. Only an impassioned appeal from Spring-Rice, in Tehran, persuaded Grey to change his mind. If the Company's steamer was forced off the river its place would be taken by foreign rivals and that would prove a serious setback to British trade in south-west Persia. Not only would British influence suffer, Spring-Rice concluded, but the £33,000 which the British government had paid in subsidies in the past would be lost. The government agreed to continue the subsidy until 1910. By then, however, the Foreign Office had lost all faith in the Euphrates and Tigris Steam Navigation Company's capacity to operate an efficient service. The Tehran legation sent home the welcomed news that other British firms would be prepared to run a steamship service on the river without any assistance from the British treasury.

Considering the importance which the government attached to the success of economic activity in southern Persia it might seem surprising that more was not done to help it. No new subsidies were paid: no financial investments were guaranteed. The closest the government actually came to spending public revenues to further British commerce was when Grey organised Treasury advances to the Persian government to keep the Swedish gendarmerie scheme alive. Formal commitments to firms operating abroad, especially when financial liability was involved, were still to be avoided. None the less, the way in which British officials advised, organised, and pressed forward railway, oil, mineral, and other interests in the area was most significant. It represented a clear break with Salisbury's rule of non-intervention in financial matters of the early 1890s. The bounds of what constituted acceptable assistance for private enterprise had been widened almost beyond recognition.

Encouragement of economic development was not the only feature of British policy in the south of Persia. It still relied on the old policy of maintaining good relations with the tribal chiefs, albeit in circumstances which, due to the Persian revolution, were more complex than before. The Bakhtiaris played an important role in the overthrow of Mohammed Ali Shah in 1909. They also dispersed the Majlis in December 1911, after which for a time they became influential in the government of the country. They had to be considered, therefore, from the viewpoint of politics at Tehran as well as simply being a bulwark against Russian expansion. A delicate balance had to be maintained. The ties which the British government had established with the chiefs of the southern tribes was not to run contrary to its obligation to preserve Persia's integrity. There could be no question of promoting separatism in the south in order to bring the tribal rulers more firmly under British protection.

In 1908 the Bakhtiari chiefs and the Sheikh of Mohammerah had both mooted the idea of a closer association with the British government; British support offered the chance of staving off encroachments on their independence by the central régime. The Foreign Office was wary of undertaking any obligations. The British government had already given certain assurances to the Sheikh of Mohammerah with respect to his independence. These could be repeated or even extended to his successor, the Foreign Office decided, but it would be impossible to guarantee him against an overland attack by Persian forces. To the Bakhtiaris no assurances had been given. The Foreign Office realised, however, that 'it would be very desirable in the interests of our trade to be on good terms with them and to have some hold over them'.[1] It was conscious of the danger that, dissatisfied with the terms of Britain's friendship, the chiefs might turn to Russia for support. Townley confirmed in 1912 that Russian influence in the southern provinces was indeed increasing. The presence of the Bakhtiari khans in Tehran during the revolution had brought them into contact with Russian diplomacy for the first time and their sympathy with Britain was less certain than before. The chiefs were sure to be impressed with Russia's authority in the north of Persia and with the fact that the Russian legation effectively nominated so many provincial governors as far south as Ispahan. 'Our Bakhtiari bulwark is becoming seriously undermined', Townley stressed: 'Russian influence in the south will seriously weaken our hold upon tribes on whose allegiance we have relied in the past'.[2] The Foreign Office therefore did its best to ensure that the chiefs were not cheated by the Anglo-Persian Oil Company with which they had made the necessary arrangements for oil exploitation in their territory. 'It is our business on political and moral grounds', an official remarked in July 1909, 'to see that the Bakhtiari khans, whose friendship is important to British interests from a general point of view, are fairly treated'.[3] A subsidy was paid to these chiefs as an inducement to keep open the road from Ahwaz to Ispahan which ran through the Bakhtiari country. Furthermore, the Foreign Office declined to give the Sheikh of Mohammerah any assurance to calm his fears of an attack on his estates by Bakhtiari tribesmen. A clerk rightly observed that 'to do so would impair our influence with the Bakhtiari for ever'.[4]

None the less Britain's relations with the Sheikh of Mohammerah

1   Minute by Norman on Marling to Grey, 23 April 1908, F.O. 371/503.
2   Townley to Grey, 20 June and 2 October 1912, *Grey Papers*, F.O. 800/70.
3   Minute by Norman on India Office to Foreign Office, 23 July 1909, F.O. 371/717.
4   Foreign Office minute on Barclay to Grey, 14 April 1910, F.O. 371/946.

were also strengthened in the late 1900s. His territory lay at the head of the Persian Gulf where the Karun River flowed into the Shatt-el-Arab. The only point of comparable importance was Kuweit. Together they were, in the words of the India Office, 'the two spots on which the feet (clay feet, possibly) of the British colossus rest in the Persian Gulf'. They had always been the centres for Britain's presence: 'they must remain and be defended unless and until we are content to abdicate in the Gulf and merely sit at its mouth'.[1] It was essential that the Sheikh of Mohammerah looked to Britain for support and friendship and not to the agents of any other foreign power.

When the Sheikh appealed for closer ties in 1908 Charles Hardinge was quick to see what might be gained. 'It is very desirable to secure his absolute adherence to our interests', he wrote to Grey, 'since he is in a position to hinder and prevent any foreign enterprises in the Karun country which might be distasteful to us or opposed to our interests'.[2] The British government confirmed its wish to uphold the status quo. This, in effect, was an assurance that the Sheikh's autonomy would be defended. The Foreign Office worked with the Sheikh in the matter of irrigation on the Karun River. The latter had his own plan which he wished to carry out; he was not particularly favourable to any foreign development. This suited the British government perfectly. Here was a means of halting any Dutch or German initiatives. Grey immediately declared that he would sanction nothing that did not have the Sheikh's approval. 'The best ground for us to take is to support the Sheikh', he remarked in 1909, 'and make his objections and our interests coincide'.[3] Foreign economic activity was barred from an important part of south-west Persia and the Sheikh was impressed with the efforts of the British government to protect him.

The ambition of the Foreign Office was to see a strong British syndicate take up the irrigation business on the Karun. This the Sheikh would surely approve since he would feel even more certain of British support if large amounts of British capital were invested in his territory. Hardinge saw the possibility as one which would materially strengthen Britain's position. Already the British owned the Bakhtiari road, the oil concession, and the right to navigate the upper Karun. A railway from Mohammerah to Khorremabad might soon become a practical

1 Minute by Hirtzel on Government of India to India Office, 11 June 1914, I.O. L/P&S/10/450, 1914, file: 2255.

2 Minute by Hardinge on Marling to Grey, 23 April 1908, F.O. 371/503.

3 Minute by Grey on India Office to Foreign Office, 27 January 1909, F.O. 371/713.

proposition and, if built, it would be a considerable asset to British trade. A big irrigation works on the Karun would combine with all these other investments to create a really strong British base around the head of the Persian Gulf. It would also 'strengthen our influence over the Sheikh', the Foreign Office observed, 'who is important in that part of the world'.[1]

The local rulers of the south thus had their place in British policy. Through them Britain's sway could be extended. Their loyalty was an integral part of the plan to create a zone of commercial and political supremacy inland from the Gulf littoral. For that reason the British government also defended its hold on the customs revenues of the Gulf ports. It continued to aid the Imperial Bank of Persia, and it did what it could to promote the growth of British trade. The Foreign Office helped British firms in undertaking the economic development of southern Persia and it blocked all other foreign enterprise from gaining a foothold in the region. In public, Grey's loyalty to the independent 'buffer state' was strong; but in reality he saw less hope of saving Persia than did his predecessors. It was no surprise, then, that Grey continued Lansdowne's efforts to strengthen British interests on the ground. The spectre of Persian integrity could be no substitute for authority in the southern provinces.

---

1   Minute by Norman on Treasury to Foreign Office, 9 December 1909, F.O. 371/719.

CONCLUSION

As with all the 'sick men' of the nineteenth century Persia's collapse was delayed far longer than expected. Throughout the period 1890 to 1914 British observers predicted a break-up of the country at any time. The truth was, as the India Office remarked back in 1906, that 'these primitive - uncivilized - nations do not perish so easily'.[1] The war completely altered things in Persia. In 1915 Britain gained control of the whole of the neutral sphere in return for acknowledging Russia's right to preponderance at Constantinople and in the Straits. Such a fortuitous arrangement, however, could not have been foreseen. Only a year previously British officials had decided that changes in their Persian policy needed to be made. The revolution in Persia and its aftermath of political instability had brought an end to all hopes that the country might somehow be set back on her feet and fulfil her role as an independent buffer state. In fact, as early as 1912, officials were again discussing the prospect of a partition of the country with Russia as the only alternative to a total collapse.

Two of the mainstays of government policy had come to little. First, the Foreign Office had supported the cause of constitutional reform with the intention that a stronger and pro-British régime replace the autocratic rule of the Kajar dynasty. By the end of 1911 it seemed certain that no such régime would emerge. Officials in London even resigned themselves to the probability that Mohammed Ali Shah would regain his throne in a counter revolution. Nicolson declared that he would no longer oppose it. The Majlis had had two years in which to prove itself but it had failed to produce a viable form of government in Tehran. British liberals had assumed that democracy was the panacea for Persia's ills; the Foreign Office had now to come to terms with the fact that representative government was quite unsuited to such a country. Nicolson no longer saw any advantage to be gained by the continuation of the Majlis. Just days before it was finally dissolved he had expressed the hope that further parliamentary experiments might be postponed for the foreseeable future. A 'strong man' was needed amid the anarchy in Persia.[2] Barclay and the legation staff shared his disillusion. 'We should certainly have been wiser to join with Russia in bolstering up Mohammed Ali than to have worked for the re-

[1] Memorandum by Barnes, 8 January 1906, I.O. L/P&S/10/9, 1903, file: 245.
[2] Nicolson to Buchanan, 5 December 1911, and Nicolson to Hardinge, 20 December 1911, *Nicolson Papers*, F.O. 800/352.

establishment of the constitution', he reflected. 'For two years we have been trying an experiment which was bound to fail'.[1]

Secondly, the British government's desire to co-operate with Russia in Persia had also yielded few results. By gaining fresh assurances from Russia concerning the integrity of Persia the 1907 Convention was designed to strengthen, not to come into conflict with, the buffer policy. By August 1914 it was clear that the attempt had not succeeded. There was much truth in what H.F.B. Lynch wrote to *The Times* in 1911: 'England and Russia are engaged in the impossible task of finding a common formula for the expression of opposite policies'.[2] The India Office and the Government of India had always hated the thought of an alliance with Russia in Central Asia. 'Seven years of bad faith' was how one senior official at the India Office described Russian behaviour between 1907 and 1914.[3] Even Nicolson, negotiator and staunchest supporter of the Russian agreement, doubted by March 1914 whether the present course could be followed for much longer. Descriptions reached him of how Russian consuls in Persia were obstructing the financial agents of the Persian government, how they gave their protection to the population who refused to pay taxes, how Persian crown lands were sold illegally, and how the Persian governors who made the sales were nothing more than Russian puppets. In May he was informed that the north of Persia had become Russian in all but name and that the process of gaining control of land and of bringing the system of tax collection under Russian control had spread into the neutral zone as far south as Ispahan.

Grey also realized that things had gone wrong. 'Our whole policy in Persia calls for reconsideration', he confessed in June 1914.[4] Charles Hardinge, though as Viceroy of India somewhat removed from the centre of diplomacy, admitted that he too now saw matters differently. The Russian government and its officials in Persia had practically ignored formal engagements to respect the sovereignty of the country. The Foreign Office would soon have to 'grasp the nettle and to face the break-up of Persia'.[5] Yet Hardinge would not concede that the 1907 Convention had been a mistake. The Russians had made

1 Barclay to Nicolson, 27 December 1911, *Nicolson Papers*, F.O. 800/353.

2 Quoted in Crewe to Hardinge, 20 October 1911, *Hardinge Papers*, vol. 73.

3 Memorandum by Hirtzel to Crewe, 27 May 1913, I.O. L/P&S/10/122, 1907, file: 2276.

4 Grey to Townley, 5 June 1914, F.O. 371/2071.

5 Memorandum by Hardinge to Cox, 6 June 1914, *Kitchener Papers, Birdwood Collection*, 1906-14, D686/50.

concessions to the terms of that understanding; without it the plight of Persia would have been more desperate still. Nicolson feared that the system of alliances in Europe was about to break down and that a Russo-German pact would dominate any new alignment of the great powers. For that reason an Anglo-Russian *entente* was still essential. 'The first principle of our foreign policy must be genuinely good relations with Russia', an official could still write in July 1914. 'For us, the fate of Persia is of necessity a secondary consideration'.[1] The fact remains, however, that only the outbreak of war saved the 1907 Convention and the nominal independence of Persia for which it had provided. Perhaps those who had always criticised that agreement were proved right in the end. Certainly Sir Mortimore Durand had foreseen this ending to any attempt to co-operate with Russia twenty years before: 'our ways are not her ways, and in the end we should probably be sorry we ever tried to work with her'.[2]

Since the late 1880s the British had tried to bring about reforms in Persia and they had tried to promote economic prosperity. The British government even lent money to the régime at Tehran in an attempt both to strengthen central authority in Persia and to lessen Persia's dependence on Russian finance. Salisbury and Lansdowne did what they could to improve relations with the Shah. Grey sided with the revolutionaries in Persia as the best hope of finding a stable authority which could hold the country together. 'Buffer state' became an acceptable term in diplomatic circles. Nicolson admitted that although it 'has hardly yet been raised to the rank of an international expression' none the less it 'is a useful phrase in conversation'.[3] It would be wrong to say that the buffer policy failed completely for, contrary to expectation, Persia remained at least nominally an independent nation in 1914. Townley complained in May that despite the tendency to ignore the existence of a Persian government at Tehran there was still such a government, 'and we are working hard to maintain that existence'.[4] By 1914, though, failure could only be a matter of time. The 1907 Convention was certainly an anachronism by then: Russian friendship and Persian integrity had proved incompatible after all. It seemed as if Salisbury's prediction in 1891 that Persia could not be 'stiffened' had been borne out by the experience of his successors in office. Disappointed and disgusted, Nicolson looked

1   Memorandum by Clerk, 21 July 1914, F.O. 371/2076.
2   Memorandum by Durand, 27 September 1895, C.P. [6704].
3   Nicolson to Hardinge, 16 May 1907, *Hardinge Papers*, vol. 10.
4   Townley to Nicolson, 13 May 1914, *Nicolson Papers*, F.O. 800/374.

back on his long association with the fortunes of that country which had begun in 1885 when he was posted to the Tehran legation: 'to my mind, no good will ever arise in Persia'.[1]

To describe the objectives of policy is not enough. The way in which the British tried to execute their Persian policy is in some respects even more important. To be able to assess policy against predetermined standards is most valuable, particularly since the British government laid down its own guide-lines. That it did not interfere in the internal affairs of independent nations and that it did not involve itself with the operations of British economic enterprise abroad had been the principles of its foreign affairs for a century before the First World War. British officials usually scanned the world with a certain sense of moral purpose. The Pax Britannica, the betterment of lesser civilizations, notions of justice, of fair play, and of propriety in international relations - this was what they had in mind when they spoke of their influence abroad. When officials used the word 'prestige' they had firm ideas of what it entailed. Prestige in Persia, a legation official remarked in 1909, 'rests largely on the honesty and justice of the officials we send there - on the brilliant reputation of the British government for disinterested humanity and fairness'.[2] It is easy to be cynical in retrospect. Of course Britain worked for her own advantage in trying to hold the Persian empire together: but in doing so her efforts surely coincided with the interests of that country. 'In the order of moral ideas we ought no doubt to stand for the independence and integrity of Persia', the India Office remarked in 1913 at a time when that policy was beginning to be questioned.[3]

However in implementing this policy officials found themselves obliged to compromise their standards of official conduct. In the first place, they could no longer keep out of Persia's domestic affairs. Lord Salisbury observed, in 1899, that 'we interfere in the Persian government to a greater extent than we do in Siam, or in China; much more than we do in the South American republics'. 'We give advice about the appointment and dismissal of governors where no British interest is concerned', he continued, 'and the complaints of the Persian government show that they at all events think they can make

1   Minute by Nicolson on Townley to Grey, 12 November 1914, F.O. 371/2060.

2   Smart to Browne, October 1908, *Browne Papers*, file: letters from Persia 1905-09.

3   Memorandum by Hirtzel to Crewe, 27 May 1913, I.O. L/P&S/10/122, 1907, file: 2276.

that accusation good'.[1] Bestowing favours and decorations on Persian officials in the early 1900s was harmless enough. The expectation nonetheless was that the British would reap some political reward by the way in which the country was governed. Sir Arthur Hardinge's efforts to sway the choice of provincial governors in the southern provinces, particularly in Seistan, went certainly beyond the bounds of ordinary diplomatic intercourse.

Likewise the close contacts which the legation established with the tribes and the petty chieftains of the south lay outside the normal channel of communication with the central régime. They were designed to serve as a safeguard for Britain's position in the Persian Gulf in the event of a collapse of authority at Tehran. Hardinge's dealings with the Persian priesthood in 1902 were, to say the least, irregular. Bribing the Mullahs at Tehran and Ispahan to stir up public agitation against a further Russian loan was a blatant attempt to use this powerful faction in Persian society to force the Shah's hand. Men such as Curzon, indeed, cared nothing even for the pretence of non-intervention. He wanted the Persian government to be told emphatically that all railway development in the south of Persia should be under British control. The British had a right to make this demand he explained in 1900. 'It is a right which we exercise all over the world, even over independent countries and governments, in matters vitally affecting our own concerns'. Curzon had no sympathy with what he saw as a belated regard for Persia's independence. 'It is not only entirely inconsistent with the whole of our policy there for 100 years, but is in conflict with what Lord Salisbury himself is saying and doing from day to day'.[2]

Curzon, as usual, overstated his case. The British did intervene in Persia, yet non-intervention remained the yardstick. Durand, at Tehran assured Salisbury in 1899 that in his view interference by the legation in internal politics was not quite as extensive as the latter seemed to believe.[3] Moreover, the Foreign Secretary had to answer to Parliament and to a mass electorate which believed in economy in public expenditure and which expected certain standards in diplomacy. Salisbury reminded Curzon in 1900, for instance, that bribery was out of the question as a means of trying to influence the Persian government: 'the maxims of British finance will not allow us to

1   Salisbury to Durand, 8 August 1899, *Salisbury Papers,* A/127.
2   Curzon to Hamilton, 4 January 1900, *Hamilton Papers,* D510/4.
3   Durand to Salisbury, 19 September 1899, *Salisbury Papers,* A/127.

compete with Russia here'.[1] In 1908 a member of the legation staff lamented the fact that British support for the Persian governor of the province of Kain had been half-hearted. The province was an important one: it bordered on Seistan. None the less Britain had allowed the pro-British governor to be ousted by a rival who was backed by Russian money and Russian intrigues chiefly because 'we did not wish to interfere in internal politics'.[2] In 1912 Nicolson reflected how any attempt by the British government to determine the factional struggles for power in Persia would be impossible. 'We should have I do not doubt a great outcry here were we to *impose* any Persian upon the country as Prime Minister'.[3]

Despite these restraints, though, during the Persian revolution the British government did favour the nationalist cause. The legation gave sanctuary to opponents of the Shah and it repeatedly urged upon the Shah the need for constitutional reform. British sympathies from the outset were with the Majlis and the government defended it against Russian intrigues. Grey managed to prevent the Russian government from giving military assistance to the old régime. He sanctioned the supply of British capital to the Shah only on condition that it should not be used to suppress the nationalist movement. In a number of ways, then, the British decided the fate of Kajar despotism and they paved the way for the attempt at constitutional government which followed. Officially Grey's policy remained one of non-intervention in Persia's internal affairs. Grey and the legation at Tehran did nothing which was overtly partisan, but they were quick to recognise and to take the opportunities available for determining the pattern of events. The British wanted a strong régime in power at Tehran and by 1906 they realised that this could be achieved only through a revolution.

The other principle in foreign affairs was that the government had no dealings with finance or commercial interests overseas. The study of Persia from 1890 to 1914 is perhaps most useful as an illustration of how change took place in that respect. This was certainly the case with financial assistance to Persia from the British treasury. Sir Arthur Hardinge rightly remarked in 1902 that any such assistance 'would be a new and difficult departure'.[4] Yet that departure occurred. The

---

1   Salisbury to Curzon, 17 October 1900, *Curzon Papers,* F111/222.

2   Cowan to Browne, 9 October 1908, *Browne Papers,* file: letters from Persia 1905-09.

3   Nicolson to Buchanan, 3 December 1912, *Nicolson Papers,* F.O. 800/360.

4   Hardinge to Lansdowne, 30 December 1902, C.P. [8377].

British government did lend money to Persia; indeed it became a matter for serious diplomatic rivalry with Russia that it should be able to do so. The reluctance of the Treasury to mix itself directly with the financing of a foreign government had been overcome by 1903. In the early 1900s Britain needed to stop the central government from falling entirely under Russian control. Throughout the period 1890 to 1914 the Foreign Office was also anxious to secure its hold over the customs administration of southern Persia and thereby to prevent any foreign interference in the Persian Gulf.

Political necessity, then, forced the government to set aside its standard of abstention from financial matters. It supported any British economic enterprise which was likely to block Russia's advance and it intervened to obstruct any that was not. In 1906 Grey wrote unequivocally that 'the broad principle upon which we must necessarily proceed is to obtain leverage over the Persian government by assisting them in a financial sense'.[1] Salisbury had tried to help the Imperial Bank of Persia to lend money to Persia in 1898-9. Lansdowne actually advanced funds from the British government in 1903 and 1904. Grey was prepared to help the Imperial Bank to issue a loan to the new regime in Persia in 1910-11 and he advanced more money from the British treasury in 1912. After 1900 the supply of foreign capital to the Persian government was always an important political consideration. Between 1906 and 1909 Grey withheld money from the Shah until the latter conceded the principle of constitutional government. After 1909, when the provision of funds became the key to the stability of the nationalist government, the Foreign Office exercised discretion as to the terms on which money should be lent and who should be allowed to lend it.

Economic concessions were also important. British officials welcomed the economic development of Persia as a precursor of political recovery and administrative reform. However they did not relish the prospect of any active promotion of British interests which might involve the government in expenditure or ultimate responsibility. But from an early date it was plain that if the Foreign Office and the Government of India wished to see the development of British economic enterprise in Persia they would have to take the initiative themselves. Apart from the years 1909 to 1911 when a number of financial firms came forward to offer money to the nationalist government Persia held out few attractions for private investors. Only in the south of Persia in the

1 Memorandum by Grey, 23 February 1906, quoted in Klein, *Historical Journal* XV (1972) p. 734.

late 1900s was there any sizable increase in British economic activity; here concessionaires took comfort from the proximity of the British navy and the assurances given by British politicians that paramountcy in the Gulf would never be surrendered.

The fact that the whole of Persia had some importance for Indian defence made no impression in the City. The sorry truth, Sir Arthur Godley observed in 1901, was that 'our interest in Persia is confined to the official classes, and even they, when they say that they care, if you ask them "Do you care to the extent of £5?" will most of them reply in the negative'.[1] Spring-Rice bemoaned the fact that economic enterprise in the country as a whole was a long record of failure and disappointment. Although officials consistently encouraged individuals and firms to invest in Persia, for most of the time their efforts were poorly rewarded. Hence the need for the subsidy of the Karun steam ship service after 1888, Curzon's efforts to stimulate trade between India and Seistan in the early 1900s, and Lansdowne's extraordinary measures to try to complete road construction in the country before 1904. Curzon admitted that he did not believe in the profitability of any of the concessions in southern Persia, but that 'it may be worth while to get hold of them for political reasons'.[2] Lord Percy, his disciple in the Foreign Office, confidently stated in 1903 that the British government should be prepared to finance concessions which were politically important. 'Once having got your stake in the form of securities on the customs or in mining, road, or oil concessions', he continued, 'you would have really earmarked a sphere on which the Russians would find it exceedingly difficult to encroach'. Certainly this involved 'an entirely new departure in policy'.[3] But Percy, like others in the small circle which determined such matters, had learned that in Persia local circumstances made a change in official attitudes essential.

This support for economic enterprise was the basis for the third major aspect of British policy - the effort to consolidate Britain's political influence in the area adjacent to the Gulf. By close relations with the tribal chiefs, by a firm hold on the southern customs, and by the extension of British trade and a proper system of communications the Foreign Office set out to create a zone across the south of Persia in which neither Russian nor German enterprise could become

1   Godley to Curzon, 13 December 1901, *Curzon Papers,* F111/150.
2   Curzon to Lansdowne, 16 March 1902, *Curzon Papers,* F111/161.
3   Percy to Curzon, 10 December 1903, *Curzon Papers,* F111/182.

established. Perhaps there was some contradiction here. The British looked to Persia as a buffer state and declared its integrity to be vital: meanwhile they were anxious to assert an exclusive claim to the south. But the Foreign Office had no difficulty reconciling these two strands of thought. The Persian Gulf was an area where British supremacy had to be defended. 'Our rights there, and our position of ascendancy', the House of Commons was told, 'We cannot abandon'.[1] No-one could be sure of preserving Persia as a buffer state for very long. The Foreign Office had to prepare for the contingency that most of the country would be absorbed by Russia and that the British would be thrown back to their sea base in the Gulf. Lord Crewe, at the India Office, summed it all up in 1912: 'If the north has to go', he wrote to the Viceroy, 'I don't see why it should be impossible to build up a buffer or barracade in the south'.[2]

The frontier of Persia had clearly failed to halt Russia's advance. Although the British clung to the 'buffer state' policy until 1914, at the same time they tried to create a new 'frontier' across the south of Persia based on economic penetration and local influence. In the late 1900s the Foreign Office supported British mineral and petroleum exploitation, irrigation works, road and telegraph enterprise, and British trade in general throughout the southern provinces way beyond the boundary of the British sphere as defined by the 1907 Convention. Even more significantly, it tried to direct the future development of railways outside the Russian sphere in opposition to both Russian and German ambitions. These were the essentials of British policy: these were the means by which the British strengthened their interests on the ground. In 1915, of course, the Foreign Office had cause for satisfaction when Russia gave over the whole of southern Persia to Britain; its holding operation there for nearly twenty years was therefore well rewarded. Russia never gained a foothold on the Persian Gulf. Even before the outbreak of war the British, in fact, were almost as secure in the south of Persia as they had been back in 1890. The war destroyed the Russian empire, but it saved the state of Persia. The British, from their point of view, had held the country together for just as long as proved necessary.

1 *Hansard* (Commons) 4th ser. CI, 613-9, 22 January 1902. Speech by Lord Cranbourne – Parliamentary Under-Secretary for Foreign Affairs.
2 Crewe to Hardinge, 5 September 1912, *Hardinge Papers*, vol. 74.

BIBLIOGRAPHY

UNPUBLISHED MATERIAL

(1) *Official Papers*

Foreign Office Records, (Public Record Office, London)
General Correspondence Series: Persia 1880-1905,   F.O. 60/...
                                    1906-1914,   F.O. 371/...

India Office Records, (India Office Library, London)
Political and Secret department L/P&S/10/...
Committee of Imperial Defence Papers L/Mil/5/...

Cabinet Papers, (Public Record Office, London)
Cabinet papers F.O. 899/...
Cabinet memoranda F.O. 899/...

(2) *Private Collections*

(a)   In the Public Record Office, London   F.O. 800/...

Papers of Lord Grey of Fallodon   (Sir Edward Grey)
Papers of Lord Hardinge of Penshurst   (Sir Charles Hardinge)
Papers of Lord Carnock   (Sir Arthur Nicolson)
Papers of Lord Sanderson   (Sir Thomas Sanderson)
Papers of the Marquess of Lansdowne
Papers of Sir Frank Lascelles
Papers of Sir Francis Villiers
Papers of Sir Cecil Spring-Rice

(b)   In the India Office Library, London

Papers of Lord Curzon of Kedleston   mss. eur. F111/...
Papers of Lord George Hamilton   mss. eur. F123/...
                                          mss. eur. C125/...
                                          mss. eur. C126/...
                                          mss. eur. D510/...
Papers of Lord Morley   mss. eur. D573/...
Papers of Lord Kitchener,
(Birdwood Collection)   mss. eur. D686/...
Papers of Sir Mortimore Durand   mss. eur. D727/...
Papers of Sir W. Lee-Warner   mss. eur. F92/...

(c)   In the University Library, Cambridge

Papers of Lord Hardinge of Penshurst   (Sir Charles Hardinge)

(d)   At Hatfield House, Hatfield, Hertfordshire

Papers of the Marquess of Salisbury

(e)   At Thriplow Bury, Thriplow, Cambridgeshire

Papers of Professor E.G. Browne

(3) *Printed Sources*

Foreign Office, Confidential Print: 1890-1914

Consular Reports for the Trade of Persia, published in Parliamentary Papers 1880-1914

Parliamentary Debates

The Banker's Magazine

S. Gwynn (ed.) *The Letters and Friendships of Sir Cecil Spring-Rice* (London, 1929)

PUBLISHED MATERIAL

Alder, G.J.	*British India's Northern Frontier 1865-95: A Study in Imperial Policy* (London, 1963)
Algar, H.	*Religion and the State in Iran 1785-1906* (California, 1969)
Avery, P.	*Modern Iran* (London, 1965)
Brockway, T.P.	'Britain and the Persian Bubble 1888-92' *Journal of Modern History* 13 (1941)
Brown, L.M.	*The Board of Trade and the Free Trade Movement 1830-42* (Oxford, 1958)
Browne, E.G.	*The Persian Revolution of 1905-09* (Cambridge, 1910)
Busch, B.C.	*Britain and the Persian Gulf 1894-1914* (California, 1967)
Churchill, R.P.	*The Anglo-Russian Convention of 1907* (Cedar Rapids, 1939)
Curzon, G.N.	*Persia and the Persian Question* (London, 1892)
Davies, C.C.	*The Problem of the North-West Frontier 1890-1908* (Cambridge, 1932)
Elwell-Sutton, L.P.	*Persian Oil: A Study in Power Politics* (London, 1955)
Entner, M.L.	*Russo-Persian Commercial Relations 1828-1914* (Florida, 1965)
Feis, H.	*Europe: The World's Banker 1870-1914* (New Haven, 1930)

148

Fieldhouse, D.K.	*Economics and Empire 1830-1914* (London, 1973)
Frechtling, L.E.	'The Reuter Concession in Persia' *Asiatic Review* 34 (1938)
Gooch, J.	'Sir George Clarke's Career at the Committee of Imperial Defence 1904-07' *Historical Journal* 18 (1975)
Graham, G.S.	*Great Britain in the Indian Ocean: A Study of Maritime Expansion 1810-50* (London, 1967)
Greaves, R.L.	*Persia and the Defence of India 1884-92* (London, 1959)
————	'British Policy in Persia 1892-1903' I and II *Bulletin of the School of Oriental and African Studies* 28 (1965)
————	'Some aspects of the Anglo-Russian Convention and its workings in Persia, 1907-1914' I and II *Bulletin of the School of Oriental and African Studies* 31 (1968)
Grenville, J.A.S.	*Lord Salisbury and Foreign Policy: the close of the Nineteenth Century* (London, 1970)
Grey, E.	*Twenty-Five Years 1892-1916* (London, 1925)
Henderson, W.O.	'German Economic Penetration in the Middle East, 1870-1914' *Economic History Review* XVIII (1948)
Imlah, A.H.	*Economic Elements in the Pax Britannica* (Cambridge, Mass. 1958)
Ingram, E.	'An Aspiring Buffer State: Anglo-Persian Relations in the Third Coalition 1804-07' *Historical Journal* 16 (1973)
Jack, M.	'The Purchase of the British Government's Shares in the British Petroleum Company 1912-14' *Past and Present* (1968)
Kazemzadeh, F.	'Russian Imperialism and Persian Railways' *Harvard Slavic Studies* 4 (The Hague, 1957)
————	*Russia and Britain in Persia 1864-1914* (London, 1968)
Keddie, N.R.	'The Origins of the Religious-Radical Alliance in Iran' *Past and Present* (1966)

'British Policy and the Iranian Opposition 1901-07' *Journal of Modern History* 39 (1967)

Kelly, J.B.   *Britain and the Persian Gulf 1795-1880* (Oxford, 1968)

Kent, M.   'Agent of Empire? The National Bank of Turkey and British Foreign Policy' *Historical Journal* 18 (1975)

Klein, I.   'The Anglo-Russian Convention and the Problem of Central Asia, 1907-14' *Journal of British Studies* 11 (1971)

————   'British Intervention in the Persian Revolution, 1905-09' *Historical Journal* 15 (1972)

Kumar, R.   *India and the Persian Gulf Region 1858-1907: A Study in British Imperial Policy* (London, 1965)

Lambton, A.K.S.   'Secret Societies and the Persian Revolution of 1905-06' *St. Antony's Papers* 14 (London, 1958)

————   'Persian Political Societies 1906-11' *St. Antony's Papers* 16 (London, 1963)

Marlowe, J.   *The Persian Gulf in the Twentieth Century* (London, 1962)

Martin, B.G.   *German-Persian Diplomatic Relations 1873-1912* (The Hague, 1959)

McLean, D.   'Commerce, Finance, and British Diplomatic Support in China 1885-6' *Economic History Review* 2nd ser. 26 (1973)

————   'Finance and "Informal Empire" before the First World War' *Economic History Review* 2nd ser. 29 (1976)

————   'English Radicals, Russia, and the Fate of Persia 1906-13' *English Historical Review* 93 (1978)

Platt, D.C.M.   *Finance, Trade, and Politics in British Foreign Policy 1815-1914* (Oxford, 1968)

Pierce, R.A.   *Russian Central Asia 1867-1917* (California, 1960)

Puryear, V.J.   *International Economics and Diplomacy in the Near East: A Study of British Commercial Policy in the Levant 1834-53* (Stanford, 1935)

Robbins, K.	*Sir Edward Grey* (London, 1971)
Ronaldshay, Earl of	*Life of Curzon* (London, 1928)
Rowland, P.	*The Last Liberal Governments* II vols (London, 1968 and 1971)
Seton-Watson, H.	*The Russian Empire 1801-1917* (Oxford, 1967)
Shuster, W.M.	*The Strangling of Persia* (London, 1912)
Steiner, Z.S.	*The Foreign Office and Foreign Policy 1898-1914* (Cambridge, 1969)
Thornton, A.P.	'British Policy in Persia 1858-1890' I *English Historical Review* 69 (1954)
————	'British Policy in Persia 1858-1890' II *English Historical Review* 70 (1955)
Trevelyan, G.M.	*The Life of John Bright* (London, 1925)
————	*Grey of Fallodon* (London, 1937)
Von Laue, T.H.	*Sergei Witte and the Industrialisation of Russia* (London, 1963)
Williams, B.J.	'The Strategic Background to the Anglo-Russian Entente of August 1907' *Historical Journal* 9 (1966)
Wolff, H.D.	*Rambling Recollections* (London, 1908)

INDEX

Abadan, 126

Admiralty, 40, 43, 46, 125, 126, 127, 128

Afghanistan, 1, 2, 14, 24, 26, 27, 32, 45, 73, 112; Amir of 4, 59

Ahwaz, 63, 64, 65, 66, 107, 116, 127, 128, 129, 134

Amin-es-Sultan, 53

Anglo-Persian oil company, 126, 127, 128, 130, 131, 134

Anglo-Persian war, 1856-7, 25

Anglo-Russian agreement in China, 41

Anglo-Russian convention of 1907, 14, 63, 70, 73-7, 83, 85, 86, 87, 101-5, 138-9, 145; and railway construction 113, 117-8, 121-2

Anglo-Russian loans to Persia, 41, 73, 84, 89, 92-3, 95, 97, 99-100, 105, 110

Anglo-Russian rivalry, 15, 114, 117-8

Arabistan, 52

Azerbaijan, 52

Bagdad railway, 23-4, 39, 86, 93, 111-3, 115, 132

Bahrein, 45

Bakhtiari, 55-6, 64-5, 90, 133-4

Balfour, Arthur James, 1st earl Balfour, 60

Baluchistan, 26, 40, 113

Banque des Prets, 18, 22, 70, 71, 77, 110

Barclay, Sir George, 81, 90, 91-2, 95, 99, 102, 117, 132, 137-8

Baring Brothers, 111

Boer war 29, 39, 40, 42, 45-6, 73

Borasjun, 129

Boulton, Messrs, 97

Boxer rebellion, 29

Britain: importance of Persia for, 19, 24, 29-30; policy in Persia 25-6, 47-8, 71, 73-4, 76, 78, 87-100, 102-5, 137-45; support for Persian constitution, 78, 81, 88-92, 137, 139, 142; support for southern tribes, 55-6, 71, 90, 133-6, 141, 144; traditions of foreign policy, 2-7, 51, 59, 87-8, 90, 92, 93-4, 100, 133, 140, 142,

'buffer state' 26-8, 29, 33, 36, 40, 42, 48, 49, 83, 121, 136, 137, 139, 145; after 1907, 75, 92, 104-5, 106, 138.

Bunder Abbas, 16, 41, 46, 47, 73, 116, 123, 124, 129, 130;

Burmah Oil Company, 126, 127

Burujird, 73

Bushire, 25, 30, 86, 107, 116

Carnock, 1st baron, *see* Nicolson, Sir Arthur

Cassel, Sir Ernest, 61, 94

156

St. Aldwyn, 1st earl, *see* Hicks-Beach, Sir Michael
Samuel, Messrs, 97
Sanderson, Sir Thomas, 1st baron Sanderson, 75
Sazanoff, S.D., 85, 86, 87, 101, 117, 118
secret service fund, 57, 58, 68-9, 115
Seistan, 108; foreign agents in, 11, 61, 73; Indian control of, 61-3, 72, 74, 113; possible British occupation of, 46-7, 75; strategic importance of, 24-5, 48, 54; support for governor of, 54-5, 61, 141
Seligman Brothers, 98-100
Shatt-el-Arab, 131, 135
Shell oil, 127
Shuster, W. Morgan, 83-4, 103, 106, 109
Siam, 45, 140
southern Persia: British policy in, 60, 63, 72, 106-36, 141, 145; disorder in, 54, 55, 107-10, 128
Spring-Rice, Sir Cecil, 78-9, 88, 104, 128, 133, 144
Strathcona, Lord, 126
Stick & Company, 130-1
subsidies 5; Amir of Afghanistan 59; Bakhtiari and Lur, 56, 134; German shipping, 23-4; Imperial Bank in Seistan, 71, 111, Karun steam-ship service, 7, 63, 68, 69, 70, 132-3; Persian Transport Company 68, 69; Swedish gendarmerie, 109-10; Tigris steamship, 7
Suez canal, 2, 4, 34
Swedish officers, 108-10, 133

Tabriz, 39, 78, 82, 89, 91, 98, 101, 103, 114
Tehran legation: attitude to Persia, 30-2; attitude to Persian loans, 33-4, 98; attitude to Russia, 75-6, 79; involvement in Persian revolution, 77, 81, 88, 142; relations with mullahs, 57-8, 72; support for Persian officials, 53-4, 71
telegraphs, 53, 61, 108, 129
Thibet, 14, 45, 73
tobacco regie, 6, 18, 56, 57
Townley, Sir Walter, 82, 90, 109, 110, 119, 122, 134, 139
trade: Anglo-Persian, 19-20, 114-5; Board of 11, 126; effect of railways on, 114, 117; German-Persian, 23-4, 115, 132; H.M.G. support of, 11, 106, 132-3, 136; Indo-Persian, 20, 62, 71, 144; Karun river trade, 72, 132; political importance of, 11, 23-4, 62, 114, 132; Russo-Persian, 20, 82, 114
Treasury, 5, 35, 115, 116, 129, 133, 142-3
trucial chiefs, 11, 23